The Law School Admission Council (LSAC) is a nonprofit corporation that provides unique, state-of-the-art admission products and services to ease the admission process for law schools and their applicants worldwide. Currently, 220 law schools in the United States, Canada, and Australia are members of the Council and benefit from LSAC's services.

LSAC fees, policies, and procedures relating to, but not limited to, test registration, test administration, test score reporting, misconduct and irregularities, Credential Assembly Service (CAS), and other matters may change without notice at any time. Up-to-date LSAC policies and procedures are available at LSAC.org.

ISBN-13: 978-0-9860862-1-2

Print number
10 9 8 7 6 5 4 3 2

TABLE OF CONTENTS

INTRODUCTION TO THE LSAT

The Law School Admission Test is a half-day standardized test required for admission to all ABA-approved law schools, most Canadian law schools, and many other law schools. It consists of five 35-minute sections of multiple-choice questions. Four of the five sections contribute to the test taker's score. These sections include one Reading Comprehension section, one Analytical Reasoning section, and two Logical Reasoning sections. The unscored section, commonly referred to as the variable section, typically is used to pretest new test questions or to preequate new test forms. The placement of this section in the LSAT will vary. A 35-minute writing sample is administered at the end of the test. The writing sample is not scored by LSAC, but copies are sent to all law schools to which you apply. The score scale for the LSAT is 120 to 180.

The LSAT is designed to measure skills considered essential for success in law school: the reading and comprehension of complex texts with accuracy and insight; the organization and management of information and the ability to draw reasonable inferences from it; the ability to think critically; and the analysis and evaluation of the reasoning and arguments of others.

The LSAT provides a standard measure of acquired reading and verbal reasoning skills that law schools can use as one of several factors in assessing applicants.

For up-to-date information about LSAC's services, go to our website, LSAC.org.

SCORING

Your LSAT score is based on the number of questions you answer correctly (the raw score). There is no deduction for incorrect answers, and all questions count equally. In other words, there is no penalty for guessing.

Test Score Accuracy—Reliability and Standard Error of Measurement

Candidates perform at different levels on different occasions for reasons quite unrelated to the characteristics of a test itself. The accuracy of test scores is best described by the use of two related statistical terms: reliability and standard error of measurement.

Reliability is a measure of how consistently a test measures the skills being assessed. The higher the reliability coefficient for a test, the more certain we can be that test takers would get very similar scores if they took the test again.

LSAC reports an internal consistency measure of reliability for every test form. Reliability can vary from 0.00 to 1.00, and a test with no measurement error would have a reliability coefficient of 1.00 (never attained in practice). Reliability coefficients for past LSAT forms have ranged from .90 to .95, indicating a high degree of consistency for these tests. LSAC expects the reliability of the LSAT to continue to fall within the same range.

LSAC also reports the amount of measurement error associated with each test form, a concept known as the standard error of measurement (SEM). The SEM, which is usually about 2.6 points, indicates how close a test taker's observed score is likely to be to his or her true score. True scores are theoretical scores that would be obtained from perfectly reliable tests with no measurement error—scores never known in practice.

Score bands, or ranges of scores that contain a test taker's true score a certain percentage of the time, can be derived using the SEM. LSAT score bands are constructed by adding and subtracting the (rounded) SEM to and from an actual LSAT score (e.g., the LSAT score, plus or minus 3 points). Scores near 120 or 180 have asymmetrical bands. Score bands constructed in this manner will contain an individual's true score approximately 68 percent of the time.

Measurement error also must be taken into account when comparing LSAT scores of two test takers. It is likely that small differences in scores are due to measurement error rather than to meaningful differences in ability. The standard error of score differences provides some guidance as to the importance of differences between two scores. The standard error of score differences is approximately 1.4 times larger than the standard error of measurement for the individual scores.

Thus, a test score should be regarded as a useful but approximate measure of a test taker's abilities as measured by the test, not as an exact determination of his or her abilities. LSAC encourages law schools to examine the range of scores within the interval that probably contains the test taker's true score (e.g., the test taker's score band) rather than solely interpret the reported score alone.

Adjustments for Variation in Test Difficulty

All test forms of the LSAT reported on the same score scale are designed to measure the same abilities, but one test form may be slightly easier or more difficult than another. The scores from different test forms are made comparable through a statistical procedure known as equating. As a result of equating, a given scaled score earned on different test forms reflects the same level of ability.

Research on the LSAT

Summaries of LSAT validity studies and other LSAT research can be found in member law school libraries and at LSAC.org.

To Inquire About Test Questions

If you find what you believe to be an error or ambiguity in a test question that affects your response to the question, contact LSAC by e-mail: LSATTS@LSAC.org, or write to Law School Admission Council, Test Development Group, PO Box 40, Newtown, PA 18940-0040.

HOW THIS PREPTEST DIFFERS FROM AN ACTUAL LSAT

This PrepTest is made up of the scored sections and writing sample from the actual disclosed LSAT administered in October 2015. However, it does not contain the extra, variable section that is used to pretest new test items of one of the three multiple-choice question types. The three multiple-choice question types may be in a different order in an actual LSAT than in this PrepTest. This is because the order of these question types is intentionally varied for each administration of the test.

THE THREE LSAT MULTIPLE-CHOICE QUESTION TYPES

The multiple-choice questions that make up most of the LSAT reflect a broad range of academic disciplines and are intended to give no advantage to candidates from a particular academic background.

The five sections of the test contain three different question types. The following material presents a general discussion of the nature of each question type and some strategies that can be used in answering them.

Analytical Reasoning Questions

Analytical Reasoning questions are designed to assess the ability to consider a group of facts and rules, and, given those facts and rules, determine what could or must be true. The specific scenarios associated with these questions are usually unrelated to law, since they are intended to be accessible to a wide range of test takers. However, the skills tested parallel those involved in determining what could or must be the case given a set of regulations, the terms of a contract, or the facts of a legal case in relation to the law. In Analytical Reasoning questions, you are asked to reason deductively from a set of statements and rules or principles that describe relationships among persons, things, or events.

Analytical Reasoning questions appear in sets, with each set based on a single passage. The passage used for each set of questions describes common ordering relationships or grouping relationships, or a combination of both types of relationships. Examples include scheduling employees for work shifts, assigning instructors to class sections, ordering tasks according to priority, and distributing grants for projects.

Analytical Reasoning questions test a range of deductive reasoning skills. These include:

- Comprehending the basic structure of a set of relationships by determining a complete solution to the problem posed (for example, an acceptable seating arrangement of all six diplomats around a table)

- Reasoning with conditional ("if-then") statements and recognizing logically equivalent formulations of such statements

- Inferring what could be true or must be true from given facts and rules

- Inferring what could be true or must be true from given facts and rules together with new information in the form of an additional or substitute fact or rule

- Recognizing when two statements are logically equivalent in context by identifying a condition or rule that could replace one of the original conditions while still resulting in the same possible outcomes

Analytical Reasoning questions reflect the kinds of detailed analyses of relationships and sets of constraints that a law student must perform in legal problem solving. For example, an Analytical Reasoning passage might describe six diplomats being seated around a table, following certain rules of protocol as to who can sit where. You, the test taker, must answer questions about the logical implications of given and new information. For example, you may be asked who can sit between diplomats X and Y, or who cannot sit next to X if W sits next to Y. Similarly, if you were a student in law school, you might be asked to analyze a scenario involving a set of particular circumstances and a set of governing rules in the form of constitutional provisions, statutes, administrative codes, or prior rulings that have been upheld. You might then be asked to determine the legal options in the scenario: what is required given the scenario, what is permissible given the scenario, and what is prohibited given the scenario. Or you might be asked to develop a "theory" for the case: when faced with an incomplete set of facts about the case, you must fill in the picture based on what is implied by the facts that are known. The problem could be elaborated by the addition of new information or hypotheticals.

No formal training in logic is required to answer these questions correctly. Analytical Reasoning questions are intended to be answered using knowledge, skills, and reasoning ability generally expected of college students and graduates.

Suggested Approach

Some people may prefer to answer first those questions about a passage that seem less difficult and then those that seem more difficult. In general, it is best to finish one passage before starting on another, because much time can be lost in returning to a passage and reestablishing familiarity with its relationships. However, if you are having great difficulty on one particular set of questions and are spending too much time on them, it may be to your advantage to skip that set of questions and go on to the next passage, returning to the problematic set of questions after you have finished the other questions in the section.

Do not assume that because the conditions for a set of questions look long or complicated, the questions based on those conditions will be especially difficult.

Read the passage carefully. Careful reading and analysis are necessary to determine the exact nature of the relationships involved in an Analytical Reasoning passage. Some relationships are fixed (for example, P and R must always work on the same project). Other relationships are variable (for example, Q must be assigned to either team 1 or team 3). Some relationships that are not stated explicitly in the conditions are implied by and can be deduced from those that are stated (for example, if one condition about paintings in a display specifies that Painting K must be to the left of Painting Y, and another specifies that Painting W must be to the left of Painting K, then it can be deduced that Painting W must be to the left of Painting Y).

In reading the conditions, do not introduce unwarranted assumptions. For instance, in a set of questions establishing relationships of height and weight among the members of a team, do not assume that a person who is taller than another person must weigh more than that person. As another example, suppose a set involves ordering and a question in the set asks what must be true if both X and Y must be earlier than Z; in this case, do not assume that X must be earlier than Y merely because X is mentioned before Y. All the information needed to answer each question is provided in the passage and the question itself.

The conditions are designed to be as clear as possible. Do not interpret the conditions as if they were intended to trick you. For example, if a question asks how many people could be eligible to serve on a committee, consider only those people named in the passage unless directed otherwise. When in doubt, read the conditions in their most obvious sense. Remember, however, that the language in the conditions is intended to be read for precise meaning. It is essential to pay particular attention to words that describe or limit relationships, such as "only," "exactly," "never," "always," "must be," "cannot be," and the like.

The result of this careful reading will be a clear picture of the structure of the relationships involved, including the kinds of relationships permitted, the participants in the relationships, and the range of possible actions or attributes for these participants.

Keep in mind question independence. Each question should be considered separately from the other questions in its set. No information, except what is given in the original conditions, should be carried over from one question to another.

In some cases a question will simply ask for conclusions to be drawn from the conditions as originally given. Some questions may, however, add information to the original conditions or temporarily suspend or replace one of the original conditions for the purpose of that question only. For example, if Question 1 adds the supposition "if P is sitting at table 2 ...," this supposition should NOT be carried over to any other question in the set.

Consider highlighting text and using diagrams. Many people find it useful to underline key points in the passage and in each question. In addition, it may prove very helpful to draw a diagram to assist you in finding the solution to the problem.

In preparing for the test, you may wish to experiment with different types of diagrams. For a scheduling problem, a simple calendar-like diagram may be helpful. For a grouping problem, an array of labeled columns or rows may be useful.

Even though most people find diagrams to be very helpful, some people seldom use them, and for some individual questions no one will need a diagram. There is by no means universal agreement on which kind of diagram is best for which problem or in which cases a diagram is most useful. Do not be concerned if a particular problem in the test seems to be best approached without the use of a diagram.

Logical Reasoning Questions

Arguments are a fundamental part of the law, and analyzing arguments is a key element of legal analysis. Training in the law builds on a foundation of basic reasoning skills. Law students must draw on the skills of analyzing, evaluating, constructing, and refuting arguments. They need to be able to identify what information is relevant to an issue or argument and what impact further evidence might have. They need to be able to reconcile opposing positions and use arguments to persuade others.

Logical Reasoning questions evaluate the ability to analyze, critically evaluate, and complete arguments as they occur in ordinary language. The questions are based on short arguments drawn from a wide variety of sources, including newspapers, general interest magazines, scholarly publications, advertisements, and informal discourse. These arguments mirror legal reasoning in the types of arguments presented and in their complexity, though few of the arguments actually have law as a subject matter.

Each Logical Reasoning question requires you to read and comprehend a short passage, then answer one question (or, rarely, two questions) about it. The questions are designed to assess a wide range of skills involved in thinking critically, with an emphasis on skills that are central to legal reasoning.

These skills include:

- Recognizing the parts of an argument and their relationships

- Recognizing similarities and differences between patterns of reasoning

- Drawing well-supported conclusions

- Reasoning by analogy

- Recognizing misunderstandings or points of disagreement

- Determining how additional evidence affects an argument

- Detecting assumptions made by particular arguments

- Identifying and applying principles or rules

- Identifying flaws in arguments

- Identifying explanations

The questions do not presuppose specialized knowledge of logical terminology. For example, you will not be expected to know the meaning of specialized terms such as "ad hominem" or "syllogism." On the other hand, you will be expected to understand and critique the reasoning contained in arguments. This requires that you possess a university-level understanding of widely used concepts such as argument, premise, assumption, and conclusion.

Suggested Approach

Read each question carefully. Make sure that you understand the meaning of each part of the question. Make sure that you understand the meaning of each answer choice and the ways in which it may or may not relate to the question posed.

Do not pick a response simply because it is a true statement. Although true, it may not answer the question posed.

Answer each question on the basis of the information that is given, even if you do not agree with it. Work within the context provided by the passage. LSAT questions do not involve any tricks or hidden meanings.

Reading Comprehension Questions

Both law school and the practice of law revolve around extensive reading of highly varied, dense, argumentative, and expository texts (for example, cases, codes, contracts, briefs, decisions, evidence). This reading must be exacting, distinguishing precisely what is said from what is not said. It involves comparison, analysis, synthesis, and application (for example, of principles and rules). It involves drawing appropriate inferences and applying ideas and arguments to new contexts. Law school reading also requires the ability to grasp unfamiliar subject matter and the ability to penetrate difficult and challenging material.

The purpose of LSAT Reading Comprehension questions is to measure the ability to read, with understanding and insight, examples of lengthy and complex materials similar to those commonly encountered in law school. The Reading Comprehension section of the LSAT contains four sets of reading questions, each set consisting of a selection of reading material followed by five to eight questions. The reading selection in three of the four sets consists of a single reading passage; the other set contains two related shorter passages. Sets with two passages are a variant of Reading Comprehension called Comparative Reading, which was introduced in June 2007.

Comparative Reading questions concern the relationships between the two passages, such as those of generalization/instance, principle/application, or point/counterpoint. Law school work often requires reading two or more texts in conjunction with each other and understanding their relationships. For example, a law student may read a trial court decision together with an appellate court decision that overturns it, or identify the fact pattern from a hypothetical suit together with the potentially controlling case law.

Reading selections for LSAT Reading Comprehension questions are drawn from a wide range of subjects in the humanities, the social sciences, the biological and physical sciences, and areas related to the law. Generally, the selections are densely written, use high-level vocabulary, and contain sophisticated argument or complex rhetorical structure (for example, multiple points of view). Reading Comprehension questions require you to read carefully and accurately, to determine the relationships among the various parts of the reading selection, and to draw reasonable inferences from the material in the selection. The questions may ask about the following characteristics of a passage or pair of passages:

- The main idea or primary purpose

- Information that is explicitly stated

- Information or ideas that can be inferred

- The meaning or purpose of words or phrases as used in context

- The organization or structure

- The application of information in the selection to a new context

- Principles that function in the selection

- Analogies to claims or arguments in the selection

- An author's attitude as revealed in the tone of a passage or the language used

- The impact of new information on claims or arguments in the selection

Suggested Approach

Since reading selections are drawn from many different disciplines and sources, you should not be discouraged if you encounter material with which you are not familiar. It is important to remember that questions are to be answered exclusively on the basis of the information provided in the selection. There is no particular knowledge that you are expected to bring to the test, and you should not make inferences based on any prior knowledge of a subject that you may have. You may, however, wish to defer working on a set of questions that seems particularly difficult or unfamiliar until after you have dealt with sets you find easier.

Strategies. One question that often arises in connection with Reading Comprehension has to do with the most effective and efficient order in which to read the selections and questions. Possible approaches include:

- reading the selection very closely and then answering the questions;

- reading the questions first, reading the selection closely, and then returning to the questions; or

- skimming the selection and questions very quickly, then rereading the selection closely and answering the questions.

Test takers are different, and the best strategy for one might not be the best strategy for another. In preparing for the test, therefore, you might want to experiment with the different strategies and decide what works most effectively for you.

Remember that your strategy must be effective under timed conditions. For this reason, the first strategy— reading the selection very closely and then answering the questions—may be the most effective for you. Nonetheless, if you believe that one of the other strategies might be more effective for you, you should try it out and assess your performance using it.

Reading the selection. Whatever strategy you choose, you should give the passage or pair of passages at least one careful reading before answering the questions. Try to distinguish main ideas from supporting ideas, and opinions or attitudes from factual, objective information. Note transitions from one idea to the next and identify the relationships among the different ideas or parts of a passage, or between the two passages in Comparative Reading sets. Consider how and why an author makes points and draws conclusions. Be sensitive to implications of what the passages say.

You may find it helpful to mark key parts of passages. For example, you might underline main ideas or important arguments, and you might circle transitional words— "although," "nevertheless," "correspondingly," and the like—that will help you map the structure of a passage. Also, you might note descriptive words that will help you identify an author's attitude toward a particular idea or person.

Answering the Questions

- Always read all the answer choices before selecting the best answer. The best answer choice is the one that most accurately and completely answers the question being posed.

- Respond to the specific question being asked. Do not pick an answer choice simply because it is a true statement. For example, picking a true statement might yield an incorrect answer to a question in which you are asked to identify an author's position on an issue, since you are not being asked to evaluate the truth of the author's position but only to correctly identify what that position is.

- Answer the questions only on the basis of the information provided in the selection. Your own views, interpretations, or opinions, and those you have heard from others, may sometimes conflict with those expressed in a reading selection; however, you are expected to work within the context provided by the reading selection. You should not expect to agree with everything you encounter in Reading Comprehension passages.

THE WRITING SAMPLE

On the day of the test, you will be asked to write one sample essay. LSAC does not score the writing sample, but copies are sent to all law schools to which you apply. According to a 2015 LSAC survey of 129 United States and Canadian law schools, almost all utilize the writing sample in evaluating some applications for admission. Failure to respond to writing sample prompts and frivolous responses have been used by law schools as grounds for rejection of applications for admission.

In developing and implementing the writing sample portion of the LSAT, LSAC has operated on the following premises: First, law schools and the legal profession value highly the ability to communicate effectively in writing. Second, it is important to encourage potential law students to develop effective writing skills. Third, a sample of an applicant's writing, produced under controlled conditions, is a potentially useful indication of that person's writing ability. Fourth, the writing sample can serve as an independent check on other writing submitted by applicants as part of the admission process. Finally, writing samples may be useful for diagnostic purposes related to improving a candidate's writing.

The writing prompt presents a decision problem. You are asked to make a choice between two positions or courses of action. Both of the choices are defensible, and you are given criteria and facts on which to base your decision. There is no "right" or "wrong" position to take on the topic, so the quality of each test taker's response is a function not of which choice is made, but of how well or poorly the choice is supported and how well or poorly the other choice is criticized.

The LSAT writing prompt was designed and validated by legal education professionals. Since it involves writing based on fact sets and criteria, the writing sample gives applicants the opportunity to demonstrate the type of argumentative writing that is required in law school, although the topics are usually nonlegal.

You will have 35 minutes in which to plan and write an essay on the topic you receive. Read the topic and the accompanying directions carefully. You will probably find it best to spend a few minutes considering the topic and organizing your thoughts before you begin writing. In your essay, be sure to develop your ideas fully, leaving time, if possible, to review what you have written. Do not write on a topic other than the one specified. Writing on a topic of your own choice is not acceptable.

No special knowledge is required or expected for this writing exercise. Law schools are interested in the reasoning, clarity, organization, language usage, and writing mechanics displayed in your essay. How well you write is more important than how much you write. Confine your essay to the blocked, lined area on the front and back of the separate Writing Sample Response Sheet. Only that area will be reproduced for law schools. Be sure that your writing is legible.

TAKING THE PREPTEST UNDER SIMULATED LSAT CONDITIONS

One important way to prepare for the LSAT is to simulate the day of the test by taking a practice test under actual time constraints. Taking a practice test under timed conditions helps you to estimate the amount of time you can afford to spend on each question in a section and to determine the question types on which you may need additional practice.

Since the LSAT is a timed test, it is important to use your allotted time wisely. During the test, you may work only on the section designated by the test supervisor. You cannot devote extra time to a difficult section and make up that time on a section you find easier. In pacing yourself, and checking your answers, you should think of each section of the test as a separate minitest.

Be sure that you answer every question on the test. When you do not know the correct answer to a question, first eliminate the responses that you know are incorrect, then make your best guess among the remaining choices. Do not be afraid to guess as there is no penalty for incorrect answers.

When you take a practice test, abide by all the requirements specified in the directions and keep strictly within the specified time limits. Work without a rest period. When you take an actual test, you will have only a short break—usually 10–15 minutes—after SECTION III.

When taken under conditions as much like actual testing conditions as possible, a practice test provides very useful preparation for taking the LSAT.

Official directions for the four multiple-choice sections and the writing sample are included in this PrepTest so that you can approximate actual testing conditions as you practice.

To take the test:

- Set a timer for 35 minutes. Answer all the questions in SECTION I of this PrepTest. Stop working on that section when the 35 minutes have elapsed.

- Repeat, allowing yourself 35 minutes each for sections II, III, and IV.

- Set the timer again for 35 minutes, then prepare your response to the writing sample topic at the end of this PrepTest.

- Refer to "Computing Your Score" for the PrepTest for instruction on evaluating your performance. An answer key is provided for that purpose.

The practice test that follows consists of four sections corresponding to the four scored sections of the October 2015 LSAT. Also reprinted is the October 2015 unscored writing sample topic.

General Directions for the LSAT Answer Sheet

The actual testing time for this portion of the test will be 2 hours 55 minutes. There are five sections, each with a time limit of 35 minutes. The supervisor will tell you when to begin and end each section. If you finish a section before time is called, you may check your work on that section **only**; do not turn to any other section of the test book and do not work on any other section either in the test book or on the answer sheet.

There are several different types of questions on the test, and each question type has its own directions. **Be sure you understand the directions for each question type before attempting to answer any questions in that section.**

Not everyone will finish all the questions in the time allowed. Do not hurry, but work steadily and as quickly as you can without sacrificing accuracy. You are advised to use your time effectively. If a question seems too difficult, go on to the next one and return to the difficult question after completing the section. **MARK THE BEST ANSWER YOU CAN FOR EVERY QUESTION. NO DEDUCTIONS WILL BE MADE FOR WRONG ANSWERS. YOUR SCORE WILL BE BASED ONLY ON THE NUMBER OF QUESTIONS YOU ANSWER CORRECTLY.**

ALL YOUR ANSWERS MUST BE MARKED ON THE ANSWER SHEET. Answer spaces for each question are lettered to correspond with the letters of the potential answers to each question in the test book. After you have decided which of the answers is correct, blacken the corresponding space on the answer sheet. **BE SURE THAT EACH MARK IS BLACK AND COMPLETELY FILLS THE ANSWER SPACE.** Give only one answer to each question. If you change an answer, be sure that all previous marks are **erased completely.** Since the answer sheet is machine scored, incomplete erasures may be interpreted as intended answers. **ANSWERS RECORDED IN THE TEST BOOK WILL NOT BE SCORED.**

There may be more question numbers on this answer sheet than there are questions in a section. Do not be concerned, but be certain that the section and number of the question you are answering matches the answer sheet section and question number. Additional answer spaces in any answer sheet section should be left blank. Begin your next section in the number one answer space for that section.

LSAC takes various steps to ensure that answer sheets are returned from test centers in a timely manner for processing. In the unlikely event that an answer sheet is not received, LSAC will permit the examinee either to retest at no additional fee or to receive a refund of his or her LSAT fee. **THESE REMEDIES ARE THE ONLY REMEDIES AVAILABLE IN THE UNLIKELY EVENT THAT AN ANSWER SHEET IS NOT RECEIVED BY LSAC.**

Score Cancellation

Complete this section only if you are absolutely certain you want to cancel your score. **A CANCELLATION REQUEST CANNOT BE RESCINDED. IF YOU ARE AT ALL UNCERTAIN, YOU SHOULD NOT COMPLETE THIS SECTION.**

To cancel your score from this administration, you **must:**

A. fill in both ovals here ...... ○ ○

AND

B. read the following statement. Then sign your name and enter the date.
YOUR SIGNATURE ALONE IS NOT SUFFICIENT FOR SCORE CANCELLATION. BOTH OVALS ABOVE MUST BE FILLED IN FOR SCANNING EQUIPMENT TO RECOGNIZE YOUR REQUEST FOR SCORE CANCELLATION.

I certify that I wish to cancel my test score from this administration. I understand that my request is irreversible and that my score will not be sent to me or to the law schools to which I apply.

_____

Sign your name in full

_____

Date

FOR LSAC USE ONLY   ●

HOW DID YOU PREPARE FOR THE LSAT?
(Select all that apply.)

Responses to this item are voluntary and will be used for statistical research purposes only.

○ By studying the free sample questions available on LSAC's website.
○ By taking the free sample LSAT available on LSAC's website.
○ By working through official LSAT *PrepTests*, *ItemWise*, and/or other LSAC test prep products.
○ By using LSAT prep books or software **not** published by LSAC.
○ By attending a commercial test preparation or coaching course.
○ By attending a test preparation or coaching course offered through an undergraduate institution.
○ Self study.
○ Other preparation.
○ No preparation.

CERTIFYING STATEMENT

Please write the following statement. Sign and date.

I certify that I am the examinee whose name appears on this answer sheet and that I am here to take the LSAT for the sole purpose of being considered for admission to law school. I further certify that I will neither assist nor receive assistance from any other candidate, and I agree not to copy, retain, or transmit examination questions in any form or discuss them with any other person.

_____
_____
_____
_____
_____
_____
_____
_____
_____

SIGNATURE: _____   TODAY'S DATE: _____ / _____ / _____
                                                                        MONTH DAY YEAR

INSTRUCTIONS FOR COMPLETING THE BIOGRAPHICAL AREA ARE ON THE BACK COVER OF YOUR TEST BOOKLET.
USE ONLY A NO. 2 OR HB PENCIL TO COMPLETE THIS ANSWER SHEET. DO NOT USE INK.

A

1 LAST NAME | FIRST NAME | MI

2 LAST 4 DIGITS OF SOCIAL SECURITY/ SOCIAL INSURANCE NO.

3 LSAC ACCOUNT NUMBER

4 CENTER NUMBER

5 DATE OF BIRTH

MONTH	DAY	YEAR
Jan		
Feb		
Mar		
Apr		
May		
June		
July		
Aug		
Sept		
Oct		
Nov		
Dec		

6 TEST FORM CODE

7 RACIAL/ETHNIC DESCRIPTION
Mark one or more
- 1 Amer. Indian/Alaska Nati
- 2 Asian
- 3 Black/African American
- 4 Canadian Aboriginal
- 5 Caucasian/White
- 6 Hispanic/Latino
- 7 Native Hawaiian/ Other Pacific Islander
- 8 Puerto Rican
- 9 TSI/Aboriginal Australia

8 SEX
- Male
- Female

9 DOMINANT LANGUAGE
- English
- Other

10 ENGLISH FLUENCY
- Yes
- No

11 TEST DATE
/ /
MONTH DAY YEAR

12 TEST FORM

Law School Admission Test

Mark one and only one answer to each question. Be sure to fill in completely the space for your intended answer choice. If you erase, do so completely. Make no stray marks.

13 TEST BOOK SERIAL NO.

SECTION 1 | SECTION 2 | SECTION 3 | SECTION 4 | SECTION 5

(Questions 1–30, answer choices A B C D E for each section)

14 PLEASE PRINT INFORMATION

LAST NAME

FIRST NAME

DATE OF BIRTH

THE PREPTEST

SECTION I

Time—35 minutes

27 Questions

<u>Directions</u>: Each set of questions in this section is based on a single passage or a pair of passages. The questions are to be answered on the basis of what is <u>stated</u> or <u>implied</u> in the passage or pair of passages. For some of the questions, more than one of the choices could conceivably answer the question. However, you are to choose the <u>best</u> answer; that is, the response that most accurately and completely answers the question, and blacken the corresponding space on your answer sheet.

"Never was anything as incoherent, shrill, chaotic and ear-splitting produced in music. The most piercing dissonances clash in a really atrocious harmony, and a few puny ideas only increase the disagreeable and
(5) deafening effect."

This remark aptly characterizes the reaction of many listeners to the music of Arnold Schoenberg. But this particular criticism comes from the pen of the dramatist August von Kotzebue, writing in 1806 about
(10) the overture to Beethoven's opera *Fidelio*.

Both Beethoven and Schoenberg stirred controversy because of the way they altered the language and extended the expressive range of music. Beethoven, of course, has stood as a cultural icon for
(15) more than a century, but that didn't happen overnight. His most challenging works did not become popular until well into the twentieth century and, significantly, after the invention of the phonograph, which made repeated listening possible.
(20) Like Beethoven, Schoenberg worked in a constantly changing and evolving musical style that acknowledged tradition while simultaneously lighting out for new territory. This is true of the three different musical styles through which Schoenberg's music
(25) evolved. He began in the late-Romantic manner— music charged with shifting chromatic harmonies— that was pervasive in his youth. People who enjoy the music of Brahms ought to love Schoenberg's *Verklaerte Nacht*, and they usually do, once they
(30) get past the fact that they are listening to a piece by Schoenberg.

Schoenberg later pushed those unstable harmonies until they no longer had a tonal basis. He did this in part because in his view it was the next inevitable step
(35) in the historical development of music, and he felt he was a man of destiny; he also did it because he needed to in order to express what he was compelled to express.

Finally, he developed the 12-tone technique as a
(40) means of bringing a new system of order to nontonal music and stabilizing it. In all three styles, Schoenberg operated at an awe-inspiring level of technical mastery. As his career progressed, his music became more condensed, more violent in its contrasts, and therefore
(45) more difficult to follow.

But the real issue for any piece of music is not how it is made, but what it has to say. If Schoenberg hadn't existed, it would have been necessary to invent him, and not because of the 12-tone system, the seeds
(50) of which appear in Mozart. What makes Schoenberg's music essential is that he precisely delineated

recognizable and sometimes disquieting emotional states that music had not recorded before. Some of his work remains disturbing not because it is incoherent,
(55) shrill, and ear-splitting, but because it unflinchingly faces difficult truths.

1. Which one of the following most accurately expresses the main point of the passage?

(A) Though Schoenberg's music is more widely appreciated today than when he was alive, it is still regarded by many as shrill and incoherent.

(B) Because of his accomplishments as a composer, Schoenberg deserves to be as highly regarded as Beethoven.

(C) Though Schoenberg's music has not always been well received by listeners, it is worthy of admiration for both its expressive range and its technical innovations.

(D) Schoenberg is most important for his invention of the 12-tone technique of musical composition.

(E) Despite the fact that he wrote at a time when recordings of his compositions were possible, Schoenberg has not been accepted as quickly as Beethoven.

2. Which one of the following could be said to be disturbing in a way that is most analogous to the way that Schoenberg's music is said to be disturbing in line 54?

(A) a comedian whose material relies heavily upon vulgar humor

(B) a comedian whose humor shines a light on aspects of human nature many people would prefer to ignore

(C) a comedian whose material is composed primarily of material already made famous by other comedians

(D) a comedian whose material expresses an extreme political philosophy

(E) a comedian whose style of humor is unfamiliar to the audience

GO ON TO THE NEXT PAGE.

3. The author begins with the quote from Kotzebue primarily in order to

(A) give an accurate account of the music of Beethoven

(B) give an accurate account of the music of Schoenberg

(C) suggest that even Beethoven composed works of uneven quality

(D) suggest that music that is at first seen as alienating need not seem alienating later

(E) suggest that one critic can sometimes be out of step with the general critical consensus

4. All of the following are similarities between Beethoven and Schoenberg that the author alludes to EXCEPT:

(A) They worked for a time in the late-Romantic style.

(B) Their music has been regarded by some listeners as incoherent, shrill, and chaotic.

(C) Their compositions stirred controversy.

(D) They worked in changing and evolving musical styles.

(E) They altered the language and expressive range of music.

5. Which one of the following aspects of Schoenberg's music does the author appear to value most highly?

(A) the technical mastery of his compositions

(B) the use of shifting chromatic harmonies

(C) the use of the 12-tone system of musical composition

(D) the depiction of emotional states that had never been captured in music before

(E) the progression through three different styles of composition seen over the course of his career

6. It can be inferred from the passage that the author would be most likely to agree with which one of the following statements about the relationships between the three styles in which Schoenberg wrote?

(A) Each successive style represents a natural progression from the previous one.

(B) Each successive style represents an inexplicable departure from the previous one.

(C) The second style represents a natural progression from the first, but the third style represents an inexplicable departure from the second.

(D) The second style represents an inexplicable departure from the first, but the third style represents a natural progression from the second.

(E) The second style represents an inexplicable departure from the first, but the third style represents a natural progression from the first.

GO ON TO THE NEXT PAGE.

The following passage was adapted from a law journal article published in 1998.

Industries that use biotechnology are convinced that intellectual property protection should be allowable for discoveries that stem from research and have commercial potential. Biotechnology researchers
(5) in academic institutions increasingly share this view because of their reliance on research funding that is in part conditional on the patentability of their results. However, questions about the extent to which biotechnology patenting is hindering basic research
(10) have recently come to the fore, and the patenting and commercialization of biotechnology inventions are now the focus of increased scrutiny by scientists and policy makers.

The perceived threat to basic research relates to
(15) restrictions on access to research materials, such as genetic sequences, cell lines, and genetically altered animals. These restrictions are seen as arising either from enforcement of a patent right or through operation of a contractual agreement. Some researchers
(20) fear that patenting biological materials will result in the patent holder's attempting or threatening to enjoin further research through a legal action for patent infringement. In other instances, a patent holder or the owner of biological materials may refuse to make such
(25) materials available to scientists conducting basic research unless a costly materials-transfer agreement or license agreement is undertaken. For example, the holder of a patent on unique biological materials may want to receive a benefit or compensation for the costs
(30) invested in the creation of the material. Academic researchers who oppose biotechnology patents fear that corporate patent holders will charge prohibitively high fees for the right to conduct basic research involving the use of patented materials.

(35) While it is true that the communal tradition of freely sharing research materials has shifted to a market model, it is also undoubtedly true that even in the early days of biotechnology, some researchers took measures to prevent competitors from gaining access
(40) to materials they had created. Scientists who resist the idea of patenting biotechnology seem to be confusing patent rights with control of access to biological materials. They mistakenly assume that granting a patent implies granting the right to deny access. In
(45) reality, whether a patent could or would be enforced against a researcher, particularly one conducting basic and noncommercial research, is questionable. First, patent litigation is an expensive endeavor and one usually initiated only to protect a market position
(50) occupied by the patent holder or an exclusive patent licensee. Second, there has been a tradition among judges deciding patent cases to respect a completely noncommercial research exception to patent infringement. Moreover, it is likely that patents will
(55) actually spur rather than hinder basic research, because patents provide scientists with a compelling incentive to innovate. Researchers know that patents bring economic rewards as well as a degree of licensing control over the use of their discoveries.

7. Which one of the following most accurately expresses the main point of the passage?

(A) By commercializing the research enterprise, biotechnology patents threaten the progress of basic research in the biological sciences.

(B) The recent shift away from a communal tradition and toward a market-driven approach to basic scientific research has caused controversy among scientists.

(C) The current system of patent protection for intellectual property unfairly penalizes both academic researchers and commercial interests.

(D) Concerns expressed by academic researchers that biotechnology patents will negatively affect their ability to conduct basic research are largely misguided.

(E) Patent litigation is so expensive that biotechnology patent holders are unlikely to bring patent-infringement lawsuits against scientists engaged in basic research.

8. The academic researchers mentioned in lines 30–31 would be most likely to subscribe to which one of the following principles?

(A) The competitive dynamics of the market should be allowed to determine the course of basic scientific research.

(B) The inventor of a biological material should not be allowed to charge fees that would prevent its use in basic research.

(C) Academic researchers should take measures to prevent their competitors from gaining access to materials they have created.

(D) Universities should take aggressive legal action to protect their intellectual property.

(E) Funding for scientific research projects should depend at least in part on the commercial potential of those projects.

GO ON TO THE NEXT PAGE.

9. According to the passage, why do university researchers increasingly believe that patents should be granted for commercially promising biotechnology discoveries?

(A) Researchers' prospects for academic advancement depend on both the quality and the quantity of their research.

(B) Researchers' funding is often contingent on whether they can produce a patentable product.

(C) Researchers see no incompatibility between unfettered basic research and the granting of biotechnology patents.

(D) Researchers increasingly believe their intellectual labor is being unfairly exploited by universities that partner with for-profit corporations.

(E) Most researchers prefer a competitive model of scientific research to a communal model.

10. With which one of the following statements would the author be most likely to agree?

(A) In the early days of biotechnology research, scientists freely shared research materials because they were not entitled to intellectual property protection for their inventions.

(B) Corporate patent holders typically charge excessive fees for the right to conduct research involving their patented materials.

(C) The cost of patent litigation is an effective check on patent holders who might otherwise try to prevent researchers engaged in basic research from using patented materials.

(D) Biotechnology researchers in academic institutions rely too heavily on funding that is partially contingent on the patentability of their results.

(E) Scientists who oppose the idea of patenting biotechnology do so because their work is not sufficiently innovative to qualify for patent protection.

11. The author refers to the early days of biotechnology (line 38) primarily in order to

(A) furnish a brief account of the evolution of academic biotechnology research

(B) establish that present competitive practices in biotechnology research are not entirely unprecedented

(C) express nostalgia for a time when biotechnology research was untainted by commercial motives

(D) argue that biotechnology research is considerably more sophisticated today than it was in the past

(E) provide a historical justification for opposition to biotechnology patents

12. The passage provides the strongest support for inferring which one of the following?

(A) Policy makers are no less likely than academic researchers to favor new restrictions on biotechnology patents.

(B) Most biotechnology patent holders believe that the pursuit of basic research in academic institutions threatens their market position.

(C) Biotechnology researchers who work in academic institutions and oppose biotechnology patents are generally unable to obtain funding for their work.

(D) Suing for patent infringement is not the only way in which patent holders can assert legal control over the use of their patented materials.

(E) Rapid commercialization in the field of biotechnology has led to a dearth of highly educated biologists willing to teach in academic institutions.

13. Suppose a university researcher wants to conduct basic, noncommercial research involving cell lines patented by a for-profit biotechnology corporation. The author would be most likely to make which one of the following predictions about the researcher's prospects?

(A) The researcher will probably be unable to use the cell lines because the corporation holding the patent will demand a prohibitively high payment for their use.

(B) The corporation holding the patent will probably successfully sue the researcher for patent infringement if she conducts the research without permission.

(C) The university that employs the researcher will likely prohibit the research in an effort to avoid being sued by the corporation holding the patent.

(D) The researcher has a good chance of not being held liable for patent infringement if she conducts the research and is subsequently sued.

(E) The corporation will probably offer to fund the research if granted exclusive rights to any resulting marketable product.

GO ON TO THE NEXT PAGE.

Before contact with Europeans, the Haudenosaune, a group of nations in northeastern North America also known as the Iroquois, had been developing a form of communication, primarily for political purposes, that

(5) used wampum, a bead carved from seashell. Most historians have insisted that wampum was primarily a form of money. While wampum certainly did become a medium of exchange among Europeans and Haudenosaune alike, this was due to the Europeans,

(10) who misinterpreted the significance of wampum and used it solely to purchase goods from the Haudenosaune. However, the true significance of wampum for the Haudenosaune lies in its gradual development from objects with religious significance into a method for

(15) maintaining permanent peace among distinct nations. Over time wampum came to be used to record and convey key sociopolitical messages.

Wampum came in two colors, white and deep purple. Loose beads constituted the simplest and oldest

(20) form of wampum. Even in the form of loose beads, wampum could represent certain basic ideas. For example, white was associated with the sky-yearning spirit, Sapling, whose terrestrial creations, such as trees, were often beneficial to humanity; deep purple

(25) was associated with Sapling's twin brother, Flint, the earth-loving spirit whose frequent mischievous vandalism (e.g., in the form of storms) often severely disrupted human life. Legend indicates, for example, that ancient Haudenosaune anglers threw the beads

(30) into the water in which they fished to communicate with Sapling or Flint (differing versions of the Haudenosaune cosmology attribute the creation of fish to one or the other of these spirits). Later, loose beads were strung together forming string wampum. It is

(35) thought that string wampum was used to send simple political messages such as truce requests.

It was, however, the formation of the Haudenosaune Confederacy from a group of warring tribes, believed by some to have occurred around 1451, that supplied

(40) the major impetus for making wampum a deliberate system of both arbitrary and pictorially derived symbols designed primarily for political purposes. This is evident in the invention of wampum belts to encode the provisions of the Haudenosaune

(45) Confederacy's constitution. These belts combined string wampum to form icons that could be deciphered by those knowing the significance of the stylized symbols. For example, longhouses, depicted in front-view outline, usually meant a particular nation

(50) of the confederacy. Council fires, possibly indicating talks in progress, were diamond outlines that could appear alone or within trees or longhouses. Lines between humanlike figures seem to have indicated the current state of relations between peoples; belts

(55) containing such images were often used as safe-conduct passes. The arrangements of the two colors also directed interpretation of the symbols. Thus, the belts served to record, store, and make publicly available items of governmental business.

(60) Although the wampum symbol system had a limited lexicon, it served to effectively frame and enforce the law of the confederacy for hundreds of years.

14. Which one of the following most accurately expresses the main point of the passage?

(A) The Haudenosaune's use of wampum originated with combinations of strings of beads with religious significance, but the need for communication between nations led to more complex uses of wampum including the transmission of political messages.

(B) For the Haudenosaune, wampum did not originally serve as a form of money but as an evolving form of communication that, through the use of colors and symbols, conveyed information and that eventually encoded the provisions of the Haudenosaune Confederacy's constitution.

(C) Wampum's significance for the Haudenosaune— as a form of communication linking their traditions with the need for the sharing of information within the confederacy—was changed through European contact so that it became exclusively a medium of commercial exchange.

(D) There is substantial evidence that the Haudenosaune's use of wampum as a medium of communication based on color combinations had its origin in the political events surrounding the establishment of the Haudenosaune Confederacy.

(E) Because of the role played by wampum in relations between the Haudenosaune and Europeans, many historians have overlooked the communicative role that bead combinations played in Haudenosaune culture prior to contact with Europeans.

15. The fishing practice mentioned in the second paragraph is offered primarily as an instance of

(A) a type of knowledge that was encoded and passed on through the use of wampum

(B) a traditional practice that was altered by contact with Europeans

(C) an activity that was regulated by the laws of the Haudenosaune Confederacy

(D) a practice that many historians learned of by studying wampum

(E) a traditional practice that reflects a stage in the evolution of wampum's uses

GO ON TO THE NEXT PAGE.

16. The last paragraph of the passage serves primarily to

(A)　detail how wampum belts evolved from other forms of wampum
(B)　distinguish between wampum belts and less complex forms of string wampum
(C)　illustrate how wampum functioned as a system of symbolic representation
(D)　outline the Haudenosaune Confederacy's constitution as it was encoded using wampum
(E)　give evidence of wampum's effectiveness as a means of ensuring compliance with the law of the Haudenosaune Confederacy

17. It can be inferred from the passage that the author would be most likely to agree with which one of the following?

(A)　Even if the evolution of wampum had not been altered by the arrival of Europeans, wampum would likely have become a form of currency because of its compactness.
(B)　The use of colors in wampum to express meaning arose in response to the formation of the Haudenosaune Confederacy.
(C)　The ancient associations of colors with spirits were important precursors to, and foundations of, later wampum representations that did not depend directly on these associations for their meaning.
(D)　Because the associations with certain colors shifted over time, the same color beads acquired different meanings on belt wampum as opposed to string wampum.
(E)　If the Europeans who first began trading with the Haudenosaune had been aware that wampum was used as a means of communication, they would not have used wampum as a medium of exchange.

18. The passage provides the most support for inferring which one of the following?

(A)　Wampum was probably used on occasion as a medium of economic exchange long before the Haudenosaune had contact with Europeans.
(B)　The formation of the Haudenosaune Confederacy called for a more complex method of communication than wampum as used until then had provided.
(C)　Once wampum came to be used as currency in trade with Europeans, the constitution of the Haudenosaune Confederacy had to be recodified using other methods of representation.
(D)　Prior to Haudenosaune contact with Europeans, wampum served primarily as a means of promulgating official edicts and policies of the Haudenosaune Confederacy.
(E)　As belt wampum superseded string wampum as a method of communication, wampum beads acquired subtler shadings in the colors used to represent abstract ideas.

19. It can be inferred from the passage that the author would be most likely to agree with which one of the following?

(A)　There is evidence that objects similar to wampum were used for symbolic representation by other peoples in addition to the Haudenosaune.
(B)　The Europeans who first came in contact with the Haudenosaune insisted on using wampum as a form of currency in spite of their awareness of its true significance.
(C)　There is evidence that Europeans who came in contact with the Haudenosaune adopted some long-standing Haudenosaune uses of wampum.
(D)　A long-term peaceful association among the groups that formed the Haudenosaune Confederacy was an important precondition for the use of wampum as a means of communication.
(E)　Present day interpretations of the significance of some of the symbols used in wampum belts are not conclusive.

GO ON TO THE NEXT PAGE.

Passage A

Karl Popper's main contribution to the philosophy of science concerns the power of negative evidence. The fundamental point is simple: No number of white swans, for example, can ever prove that all swans are
(5) white, but a single black swan disproves the hypothesis. Popper gives this logical asymmetry between positive and negative evidence hyperbolic application, maintaining that positive evidence has no value as evidence and that negative evidence is tantamount to
(10) disproof. Moreover, Popper takes the search for negative evidence to be at the heart of scientific research; that is, for Popper, scientific research involves not only generating bold theories, but also searching for evidence that would disprove them.
(15) Indeed, for him, a theory counts as scientific only if it makes predictions that are testable in this way.

However, Popper's use of the logical asymmetry does not adequately capture the actual situation scientists face. If a theory deductively entails a false
(20) prediction, then the theory must be false as well. But a scientific theory rarely entails predictions on its own. When scientists actually derive a theory's predictions, they almost always need diverse additional "auxiliary" premises, which appeal to other theories, to the correct
(25) functioning of instrumentation, to the absence of disturbing forces, etc. When a prediction fails, logic indicates that at least one of the premises must be false, but it does not indicate which one. When an experiment does not work out as predicted, there is
(30) usually more than one possible explanation. Positive evidence is never conclusive. But negative evidence rarely is either.

Passage B

When the planet Uranus was discovered, astronomers attempted to predict its orbit. They based
(35) their predictions on Newton's laws and auxiliary assumptions about the mass of the sun and the masses, orbits, and velocities of other planets. One of the auxiliary assumptions was that no planets existed in the vicinity of Uranus. When the astronomers made
(40) their observations, they found that the orbit they had predicted for Uranus was incorrect. One possible explanation for the failure of their prediction was that Newton's laws were incorrect. Another was that there was an error in the auxiliary assumptions. The
(45) astronomers changed their assumptions about the existence of other planets, concluding that there must be another planet close enough to Uranus to produce the observed orbit. Not long afterward, scientists discovered the planet Neptune in the precise place it
(50) would have to be to bring their calculations into alignment with their observations.

Later astronomers, again using Newton's laws, predicted the orbit of Mercury. Once again, the predictions were not borne out. They hypothesized the
(55) existence of another planet in the vicinity, which they called Vulcan. However, Vulcan was never found, and some scientists began to think that perhaps Newton's laws were in error. Finally, when Einstein's general theory of relativity was introduced, astronomers

(60) discovered that calculations based on that theory and the old auxiliary assumptions predicted the observed orbit of Mercury, leading to the rejection of Newton's theory of gravity and to increased confidence in Einstein's theory.

20. Which one of the following is a central topic of both passages?

    (A) the logical asymmetry of positive and negative evidence
    (B) the role of auxiliary assumptions in predicting planetary orbits
    (C) the role of negative evidence in scientific research
    (D) the proper technique for confirming a scientific theory
    (E) the irrelevance of experimentation for disproving a scientific theory

21. Which one of the following is mentioned in passage A and illustrated in passage B?

    (A) repudiating an experimental result
    (B) revising a theory
    (C) disproving a theory
    (D) predicting a planet's orbit
    (E) theories that are not testable by experiment

22. In passage B, which one of the following most clearly illustrates a disturbing force, as described in passage A (line 26)?

    (A) Uranus
    (B) the sun
    (C) Neptune
    (D) Mercury
    (E) the moon

23. In saying that Popper gives a certain idea "hyperbolic application" (line 7), the author of passage A means to suggest that Popper

    (A) extends the idea to cases in which it does not apply
    (B) underestimates the significance of the idea
    (C) commits a logical fallacy in reasoning about the idea
    (D) draws too radical a conclusion from the idea
    (E) exaggerates the idea's relevance to a particular theory

GO ON TO THE NEXT PAGE.

24. The author of passage A would be most likely to take which one of the following results mentioned in passage B as support for the claim made in the last sentence of passage A?

   (A) the discovery of Uranus
   (B) the initial failure of Newton's laws to correctly predict Uranus's orbit
   (C) the ultimate failure of Newton's laws to correctly predict Mercury's orbit
   (D) the failure to find Vulcan
   (E) the success of Einstein's general theory of relativity at predicting Mercury's orbit

25. In passage B's description of the developments leading to the rejection of Newton's theory of gravity, which one of the following astronomical bodies plays a role most analogous to the black swan discussed in passage A?

   (A) Mercury
   (B) Uranus
   (C) Neptune
   (D) Venus
   (E) the sun

26. It can be inferred that the author of passage B would be likely to be most skeptical of which one of the following ideas mentioned in passage A?

   (A) Popper's main contribution to the philosophy of science concerned the power of negative evidence.
   (B) Positive evidence plays no role in supporting a theory.
   (C) Auxiliary premises are usually needed in order to derive predictions from a scientific theory.
   (D) There is a logical asymmetry between positive and negative evidence.
   (E) Scientific research involves generating bold theories and attempting to refute them.

27. Which one of the following scientific episodes is most analogous to the discovery of Neptune, as that episode is described in passage B?

   (A) Galileo proposed that ocean tides are the result of Earth's motion in its orbit around the sun. But Galileo's theory of tides falsely predicted that there is only one high tide per day, when in fact there are two.
   (B) By observing "variable stars"—stars that vary in brightness—in Andromeda, Edwin Hubble discovered that Andromeda is actually a galaxy in its own right. This enabled him to settle the debate about whether the Milky Way constitutes the entirety of the universe.
   (C) Walter Alvarez postulated that an asteroid impact caused the extinction of the dinosaurs. He based this on observing high levels of the mineral iridium in certain rock core samples. Later evidence of a large impact crater was discovered in the Yucatan Peninsula that dates to the time of the dinosaur extinction.
   (D) Bernard Brunhes discovered rocks that were magnetized in a direction opposite to that of the present-day magnetic field. He concluded that Earth's magnetic field must have been reversed at some point in the past.
   (E) When a neutron decays into a proton and an electron, the combined energies of the two particles is less than the energy of the original neutron, in apparent contradiction of the law of conservation of energy. Wolfgang Pauli postulated that a third undetected particle is also created during the decay. The particle's existence was later confirmed.

S T O P

IF YOU FINISH BEFORE TIME IS CALLED, YOU MAY CHECK YOUR WORK ON THIS SECTION ONLY.
DO NOT WORK ON ANY OTHER SECTION IN THE TEST.

SECTION II

Time—35 minutes

26 Questions

Directions: The questions in this section are based on the reasoning contained in brief statements or passages. For some questions, more than one of the choices could conceivably answer the question. However, you are to choose the best answer; that is, the response that most accurately and completely answers the question. You should not make assumptions that are by commonsense standards implausible, superfluous, or incompatible with the passage. After you have chosen the best answer, blacken the corresponding space on your answer sheet.

1. In the bodies of reptiles, some industrial by-products cause elevated hormonal activity. Hormones govern the development of certain body parts, and in reptiles abnormal development of these parts occurs only with elevated hormonal activity. Recently, several alligators with the telltale developmental abnormalities were discovered in a swamp. So, apparently, industrial by-products have entered the swamp's ecosystem.

The reasoning in the argument is most vulnerable to criticism on the grounds that the argument

(A) provides no explanation for developmental abnormalities that do not result from elevated hormonal activity

(B) fails to consider whether elevated hormonal activity can result from factors other than the presence of industrial by-products

(C) fails to address the possibility that industrial by-products were contained in food the alligators ate

(D) fails to say whether reptiles other than alligators were examined for the same developmental abnormalities that were discovered in the alligators

(E) uses evidence drawn from a sample of alligators that is unlikely to be representative of alligators in general

2. Government official: Residents who are foreign citizens can serve as public servants at most levels, but not as cabinet secretaries. This is wise, since cabinet secretaries perform some duties that should be performed only by citizens, and no one should be appointed to a position if it involves duties that person should not perform. Moreover, a cabinet undersecretary is expected to serve as cabinet secretary when the actual secretary is unavailable. So, _____.

Which one of the following most logically completes the government official's statement?

(A) foreign citizens who serve as public servants should be granted citizenship in the country they serve

(B) foreign citizens should not be appointed as cabinet undersecretaries

(C) only former cabinet undersecretaries should be appointed as cabinet secretaries

(D) foreign citizens should be eligible to serve as cabinet secretaries

(E) cabinet undersecretaries should not be expected to stand in for cabinet secretaries

GO ON TO THE NEXT PAGE.

3. Doris: I've noticed that everyone involved in student government is outspoken. So if we want students to be more outspoken, we should encourage them to become involved in student government.

Zack: Those who are in student government became involved precisely because they are outspoken in the first place. Encouraging others to become involved will do nothing to make them more outspoken.

Doris and Zack disagree over whether

(A)   students should be more outspoken
(B)   students should be encouraged to become involved in student government
(C)   becoming involved in student government makes students more outspoken
(D)   all students who are involved in student government are outspoken
(E)   students will not become more outspoken unless they become involved in student government

4. Biologist: A careful study of the behavior of six individual chameleons concluded that lizards such as chameleons bask in the sun not only for warmth but also to regulate their production of vitamin D. Critics of the study—although correct in observing that its sample size was very small—are wrong to doubt its results. After all, the study's author is well regarded professionally and has been doing excellent work for years.

The reasoning in the biologist's argument is most vulnerable to criticism on the grounds that the argument

(A)   takes the behavior of chameleons to be generalizable to lizards as a whole
(B)   fails to explain how chameleons regulate their vitamin D production by basking in the sun
(C)   focuses its attention on the study's author rather than on the study itself
(D)   fails to demonstrate that the study's critics have relevant expertise
(E)   holds the study's author to a higher standard than it holds the study's critics

5. Political scientist: Some analysts point to the government's acceptance of the recent protest rally as proof that the government supports freedom of popular expression. But the government supports no such thing. Supporting freedom of popular expression means accepting the expression of ideas that the government opposes as well as the expression of ideas that the government supports. The message of the protest rally was one that the government entirely supports.

Which one of the following is an assumption that is required by the political scientist's argument?

(A)   The government helped to organize the recent protest rally.
(B)   The message of the recent protest rally did not concern any function of the government.
(C)   The government would not have accepted a protest rally whose message it opposed.
(D)   There are groups that are inhibited from staging a protest rally out of a fear of government response.
(E)   The government feared a backlash if it did not show acceptance of the recent protest rally.

6. Lawyer: In addition to any other penalties, convicted criminals must now pay a "victim surcharge" of $30. The surcharge is used to fund services for victims of violent crimes, but this penalty is unfair to nonviolent criminals since the surcharge applies to all crimes, even nonviolent ones like petty theft.

Which one of the following principles, if valid, would most help to justify the reasoning in the lawyer's argument?

(A)   The penalties for a crime should be severe enough to deter most people who would commit the crime if there were no penalties.
(B)   The overall penalty for a violent crime should be more severe than the overall penalty for any nonviolent crime.
(C)   A surcharge intended to provide services to victims is justified only if all proceeds of the surcharge are used to provide services.
(D)   A criminal should not be required to pay for services provided to victims of crimes that are more serious than the type of crime the criminal has been convicted of.
(E)   Convicted thieves should be fined an amount at least as great as the value of the property stolen.

GO ON TO THE NEXT PAGE.

7. Economist: Owing to global economic forces since 1945, our country's economy is increasingly a service economy, in which manufacturing employs an ever smaller fraction of the workforce. Hence, we have engaged in less and less international trade.

Which one of the following, if true, would most help to explain the decreasing engagement in international trade by the economist's country?

(A) International trade agreements have usually covered both trade in manufactured goods and trade in services.
(B) Employment in the service sector tends to require as many specialized skills as does employment in manufacturing.
(C) Because services are usually delivered in person, markets for services tend to be local.
(D) Many manufacturing jobs have been rendered obsolete by advances in factory automation.
(E) Some services can be procured less expensively from providers in other countries than from providers in the economist's country.

8. Merton: A study showed that people who live on very busy streets have higher rates of heart disease than average. I conclude that this elevated rate of heart disease is caused by air pollution from automobile exhaust.

Ortiz: Are you sure? Do we know whether people living on busy streets have other lifestyle factors that are especially conducive to heart disease?

Ortiz criticizes Merton's argument by

(A) raising a question about the validity of the study that Merton cites
(B) contending that Merton needs to take into account other effects of air pollution
(C) claiming that Merton misunderstands a crucial aspect of the study's findings
(D) raising a counterexample to the general conclusion that Merton draws
(E) suggesting that alternative explanations for the study's findings need to be ruled out

9. Two lakes in the Pawpaw mountains, Quapaw and Highwater, were suffering from serious declines in their fish populations ten years ago. Since that time, there has been a moratorium on fishing at Quapaw Lake, and the fish population there has recovered. At Highwater Lake, no such moratorium has been imposed, and the fish population has continued to decline. Thus, the ban on fishing is probably responsible for the rebound in the fish population at Quapaw Lake.

Which one of the following, if true, most seriously weakens the argument above?

(A) Highwater Lake is in an area of the mountains that is highly susceptible to acid rain.
(B) Prior to the ban, there was practically no fishing at Quapaw Lake.
(C) Highwater Lake is much larger than Quapaw Lake.
(D) Several other lakes in the Pawpaw mountains have recently had increases in their fish populations.
(E) There used to be a greater variety of fish species in Highwater Lake than in Quapaw Lake, but there no longer is.

10. The Asian elephant walks with at least two, and sometimes three, feet on the ground at all times. Even though it can accelerate, it does so merely by taking quicker and longer steps. So the Asian elephant does not actually run.

The conclusion drawn above follows logically if which one of the following is assumed?

(A) If an animal cannot accelerate, then it cannot run.
(B) To run, an animal must have all of its feet off the ground at once.
(C) The Asian elephant can walk as quickly as some animals run.
(D) It is unusual for a four-legged animal to keep three feet on the ground while walking.
(E) All four-legged animals walk with at least two feet on the ground at all times.

GO ON TO THE NEXT PAGE.

11. A hardware store generally sells roughly equal numbers of Maxlast brand hammers and Styron brand hammers. Last week, all of the Maxlast hammers were put on sale and placed in a display case just inside the store entrance while the Styron hammers retained their usual price and location. Surprisingly, the Styron hammers slightly outsold the Maxlast hammers.

Which one of the following, if true, does most to explain the surprising result?

(A) For the first several seconds after shoppers enter a store, they do not take detailed notice of the store's merchandise.

(B) Most of the hardware store's customers are attracted by quality and service rather than low prices.

(C) Customers who bought the Maxlast hammers last week commonly mentioned the sale as their reason for buying a hammer at that time.

(D) The hardware store circulated flyers that publicized the sale prices on Maxlast hammers.

(E) In general, a single item that is on sale will not motivate shoppers to make a special trip to a store.

12. In an experiment, two groups of mice—one whose diet included ginkgo extract and one that had a normal diet—were taught to navigate a maze. The mice whose diet included ginkgo were more likely to remember how to navigate the maze the next day than were the other mice. However, the ginkgo may not have directly enhanced memory. Other studies have found that ginkgo reduces stress in mice, and lowering very high stress levels is known to improve recall.

Which one of the following, if true, would most weaken the argument?

(A) The doses of ginkgo in the diet of the mice in the experiment were significantly higher than the doses that have been shown to reduce stress in mice.

(B) Neither the mice who received the ginkgo nor the other mice in the experiment exhibited physiological signs of higher-than-normal stress.

(C) Some chemical substances that reduce stress in mice also at least temporarily impair their memory.

(D) Scientists have not yet determined which substances in ginkgo are responsible for reducing stress in mice.

(E) The mice who received the ginkgo took just as long as the other mice to learn to navigate the maze.

13. Some of the politicians who strongly supported free trade among Canada, the United States, and Mexico are now refusing to support publicly the idea that free trade should be extended to other Latin American countries.

If the statement above is true, which one of the following must also be true?

(A) Some of the politicians who now publicly support extending free trade to other Latin American countries did not support free trade among Canada, the United States, and Mexico.

(B) Not all politicians who now publicly support extending free trade to other Latin American countries strongly supported free trade among Canada, the United States, and Mexico.

(C) Some of the politicians who strongly supported free trade among Canada, the United States, and Mexico have changed their position on free trade.

(D) Not all politicians who strongly supported free trade among Canada, the United States, and Mexico now publicly support extending free trade to other Latin American countries.

(E) Some of the politicians who strongly supported free trade among Canada, the United States, and Mexico now publicly oppose extending free trade to other Latin American countries.

GO ON TO THE NEXT PAGE.

14. Principle: Any person or business knowingly aiding someone's infringement on a copyright is also guilty of copyright infringement.

    Application: Grandview Department Store, which features a self-service photo-printing kiosk, is guilty of copyright infringement since a customer using the kiosk infringed on a wedding photographer's copyright by printing photographs whose copyright is held by the photographer.

    Which one of the following, if assumed, most helps to justify the application of the principle?

    (A) The operator of a business has the same legal obligations to customers who use self-service facilities as it has to customers who use full-service facilities.
    (B) The management of a business that is open to the public is obligated to report to the authorities any illegal activity that it witnesses on its property.
    (C) The owner of a self-service printing kiosk should post a notice advising customers that copyrighted material should not be printed at the kiosk without the permission of the copyright holder.
    (D) Owners of self-service facilities should monitor those facilities in order to ensure that they are not used for illegal or unethical purposes.
    (E) A person or business providing a service that can be expected to be used to infringe on a copyright should be considered to knowingly aid any copyright infringer using the service.

15. Journalism's purpose is to inform people about matters relevant to the choices they must make. Yet, clearly, people often buy newspapers or watch television news programs precisely because they contain sensationalistic gossip about people whom they will never meet and whose business is of little relevance to their lives. Obviously, then, the sensationalistic gossip contained in newspapers and television news programs _____.

    Which one of the following most logically completes the argument?

    (A) is at least sometimes included for nonjournalistic reasons
    (B) prevents those news media from achieving their purpose
    (C) is more relevant to people's lives now than it used to be
    (D) should not be thought of as a way of keeping an audience entertained
    (E) is of no value to people who are interested in journalism

16. When surveyed about which party they would like to see in the legislature, 40 percent of respondents said Conservative, 20 percent said Moderate, and 40 percent said Liberal. If the survey results are reliable, we can conclude that most citizens would like to see a legislature that is roughly 40 percent Conservative, 20 percent Moderate, and 40 percent Liberal.

    Which one of the following most accurately describes a flaw in the reasoning of the argument?

    (A) The argument uses premises about the actual state of affairs to draw a conclusion about how matters should be.
    (B) The argument draws a conclusion that merely restates a premise presented in favor of it.
    (C) The argument takes for granted that the preferences of a group as a whole are the preferences of most individual members of the group.
    (D) The argument fails to consider that the survey results might have been influenced by the political biases of the researchers who conducted the survey.
    (E) The argument uses evidence that supports only rough estimates to draw a precisely quantified conclusion.

GO ON TO THE NEXT PAGE.

17. City leader: If our city adopts the new tourism plan, the amount of money that tourists spend here annually will increase by at least $2 billion, creating as many jobs as a new automobile manufacturing plant would. It would be reasonable for the city to spend the amount of money necessary to convince an automobile manufacturer to build a plant here, but adopting the tourism plan would cost less.

The city leader's statements, if true, provide the most support for which one of the following?

(A) The city should implement the least expensive job creation measures available.

(B) In general, it is reasonable for the city to spend money to try to convince manufacturing companies to build plants in the city.

(C) The city cannot afford both to spend money to convince an automobile manufacturer to build a plant in the city and to adopt the new tourism plan.

(D) It would be reasonable for the city to adopt the new tourism plan.

(E) The only way the city can create jobs is by increasing tourism.

18. An article claims that many medical patients have an instinctual ability to predict sudden changes in their medical status. But the evidence given is anecdotal and should not be trusted. The case is analogous to empirically disproven reports that babies are born in disproportionately high numbers during full moons. Once that rumor became popular, maternity room staff were more likely to remember busy nights with full moons than busy nights without them.

The argument requires the assumption that

(A) the article claiming that medical patients can instinctually predict sudden changes in their medical status will soon be empirically disproven

(B) patients' predictions of sudden changes in their medical status are less likely to be remembered by medical staff if no such change actually occurs

(C) the patients in the article were not being serious when they predicted sudden changes in their medical status

(D) babies are less likely to be born during a night with a full moon than during a night without a full moon

(E) the idea that medical patients have an instinctual ability to predict sudden changes in their medical status is not a widely held belief

19. Politician: Union leaders argue that increases in multinational control of manufacturing have shifted labor to nations without strong worker protections, resulting in a corresponding global decrease in workers' average wages. Given that these leaders have a vested interest in seeing wages remain high, they would naturally want to convince legislators to oppose multinational control. Thus, legislators should reject this argument.

The reasoning in the politician's argument is flawed in that the argument

(A) treats the mere fact that certain people are union members as sufficient to cast doubt on all of the viewpoints expressed by those people

(B) presumes, without providing justification, that anyone whose political motivations are clearly discernible is an unreliable source of information to legislators

(C) treats circumstances potentially affecting the union leaders' argument as sufficient to discredit those leaders' argument

(D) presumes, without providing justification, that the argument it cites is the union leaders' only argument for their view

(E) presumes, without providing evidence, that leaders of all unions argue against increases in multinational control of manufacturing

20. Professor: The number of new university students who enter as chemistry majors has not changed in the last ten years, and job prospects for graduates with chemistry degrees are better than ever. Despite this, there has been a significant decline over the past decade in the number of people earning chemistry degrees.

Which one of the following, if true, most helps to explain the decline?

(A) Many students enter universities without the academic background that is necessary for majoring in chemistry.

(B) There has been a significant decline in the number of undergraduate degrees earned in the natural sciences as a whole.

(C) Many students are very unsure of their choice when they pick a major upon entering universities.

(D) Job prospects for graduates with chemistry degrees are no better than prospects for graduates with certain other science degrees.

(E) Over the years, first-year chemistry has come to be taught in a more routinely methodical fashion, which dampens its intellectual appeal.

GO ON TO THE NEXT PAGE.

21. Although the first humans came to Australia 56,000 years ago and undoubtedly brought new diseases with them, human-borne diseases probably did not cause the mass extinction of large land animals and birds that took place over the following 10,000 years. After all, more than 55 different species disappeared at about the same time, and no one disease, however virulent, could be fatal to animals across that many different species.

Which one of the following arguments exhibits flawed reasoning that is most parallel to that in the argument above?

(A) Even though high interest rates can lead to an economic downturn, high interest rates probably did not cause the current economic downturn. It is true that rates have been on the rise, but high interest rates are not always economically harmful.

(B) Even though I can fix some things and you can fix some things, the two of us will be unable to repair our apartment without outside help. The apartment has both a broken window and a broken bedroom door, and neither of us is able to fix both doors and windows.

(C) Even though Lena, Jen, and Mark would like to go out to dinner together after the movie tonight, they will probably go straight home after the show. Of the five restaurants that are in the immediate vicinity of the theater, there is not a single one that all three of them like.

(D) Even though this painting is highly regarded by critics, it cannot legitimately be deemed great art. Most art that was produced in the last hundred years is not great art, and this painting, beautiful though it is, was probably painted only 40 years ago.

(E) Even though the influenza vaccine does not always prevent influenza, it sometimes reduces the severity of its symptoms. Therefore it is incorrect to say that some people who receive the vaccine derive no benefit from it.

22. A tax preparation company automatically adds the following disclaimer to every e-mail message sent to its clients: "Any tax advice in this e-mail should not be construed as advocating any violation of the provisions of the tax code." The only purpose this disclaimer could serve is to provide legal protection for the company. But if the e-mail elsewhere suggests that the client do something illegal, then the disclaimer offers no legal protection. So the disclaimer serves no purpose.

The argument's conclusion can be properly drawn if which one of the following is assumed?

(A) If the e-mail does not elsewhere suggest that the client do anything illegal, then the company does not need legal protection.

(B) If e-mail messages sent by the tax preparation company do elsewhere suggest that the recipient do something illegal, then the company could be subject to substantial penalties.

(C) A disclaimer that is included in every e-mail message sent by a company will tend to be ignored by recipients who have already received many e-mails from that company.

(D) At least some of the recipients of the company's e-mails will follow the advice contained in the body of at least some of the e-mails they receive.

(E) Some of the tax preparation company's clients would try to illegally evade penalties if they knew how to do so.

23. Well-intentioned people sometimes attempt to resolve the marital problems of their friends. But these attempts are usually ineffectual and thereby foster resentment among all parties. Thus, even well-intentioned attempts to resolve the marital problems of friends are usually unjustified.

Which one of the following principles, if valid, most strongly supports the reasoning above?

(A) One should get involved in other people's problems only with the intention of producing the best overall consequences.

(B) Interpersonal relations should be conducted in accordance with doing whatever is right, regardless of the consequences.

(C) Good intentions are the only legitimate grounds on which to attempt to resolve the marital problems of friends.

(D) The intentions of an action are irrelevant to whether or not that action is justified.

(E) No actions based on good intentions are justified unless they also result in success.

24. It has been said that authors who write in order to give pleasure cannot impart to their readers the truth of their subject matter. That claim cannot be true. If it were, one could determine the truthfulness of a book simply by looking at its sales figures. If the book were very popular, one could reasonably conclude that it gave people pleasure and therefore that at least some of what is written in the book is not true.

Which one of the following is an assumption required by the argument?

(A) When people choose to read a book, they generally do not already know whether reading it will give them pleasure.

(B) Even when an author writes with the goal of giving people pleasure, that goal will not necessarily be achieved.

(C) In many cases, a book's readers are unconcerned about the truth of the book's contents.

(D) A book will not give its readers pleasure unless it was intended by its author to have that effect.

(E) A book can be popular for reasons other than its ability to give readers pleasure.

25. It is likely that most of the new television programs Wilke & Wilke produce for this season will be canceled. Most of the new shows they produced last season were canceled due to insufficient viewership. Furthermore, their new shows are all police dramas, and few police dramas have been popular in recent years.

Which one of the following, if true, most helps to strengthen the argument?

(A) Wilke & Wilke have produced more new shows for this season than they produced last season.

(B) Most of the shows that Wilke & Wilke produced last year were police dramas.

(C) None of the shows that Wilke & Wilke produced last year that were not canceled were police dramas.

(D) All of the new shows that Wilke & Wilke produced last year that were canceled were police dramas.

(E) None of the most popular television shows last year were police dramas.

26. If a corporation obtains funds fraudulently, then the penalty should take into account the corporation's use of those funds during the time it held them. In such cases, the penalty should completely offset any profit the corporation made in using the funds.

Which one of the following conforms most closely to the principle illustrated above?

(A) If a driver causes an accident because the automobile being driven was not properly maintained, that driver should be required from then on to regularly demonstrate that his or her automobile is being properly maintained.

(B) If a factory is found to have been recklessly violating pollution laws, that factory should be required to make the expenditures necessary to bring it into compliance with those laws to the satisfaction of the regulators.

(C) If someone is sentenced to perform community service, the court has a responsibility to ensure that the community at large rather than a private group benefits from that service.

(D) If an athlete is found to have used banned performance-enhancing substances, that athlete should be prohibited from participating in all future athletic competitions.

(E) If a convicted criminal writes a memoir describing the details of that criminal's crime, any proceeds of the book should be donated to a charity chosen by a third party.

S T O P

IF YOU FINISH BEFORE TIME IS CALLED, YOU MAY CHECK YOUR WORK ON THIS SECTION ONLY.
DO NOT WORK ON ANY OTHER SECTION IN THE TEST.

SECTION III

Time—35 minutes

23 Questions

Directions: Each group of questions in this section is based on a set of conditions. In answering some of the questions, it may be useful to draw a rough diagram. Choose the response that most accurately and completely answers each question and blacken the corresponding space on your answer sheet.

Questions 1–6

A detective is trying to determine the order in which a criminal recruited seven accomplices—Peters, Quinn, Rovero, Stanton, Tao, Villas, and White. In addition to discovering that the suspect recruited the accomplices one at a time, the detective has established the following:

    Stanton was recruited neither immediately before nor immediately after Tao.

    Quinn was recruited earlier than Rovero.

    Villas was recruited immediately before White.

    Peters was recruited fourth.

1. Which one of the following could be the order in which the accomplices were recruited, from first to last?

  (A)   Quinn, Tao, Stanton, Peters, Villas, White, Rovero

  (B)   Quinn, White, Rovero, Peters, Stanton, Villas, Tao

  (C)   Villas, White, Quinn, Stanton, Peters, Tao, Rovero

  (D)   Villas, White, Stanton, Peters, Quinn, Tao, Rovero

  (E)   Villas, White, Stanton, Peters, Rovero, Tao, Quinn

GO ON TO THE NEXT PAGE.

2. Which one of the following could be the list of the middle five accomplices, in the order in which they were recruited, from second to sixth?

    (A)   Quinn, Stanton, Peters, Tao, Villas
    (B)   Quinn, Stanton, Peters, Tao, White
    (C)   Villas, White, Peters, Quinn, Stanton
    (D)   Villas, White, Peters, Rovero, Stanton
    (E)   Villas, White, Quinn, Rovero, Stanton

3. If Tao was recruited second, which one of the following could be true?

    (A)   Quinn was recruited third.
    (B)   Rovero was recruited fifth.
    (C)   Stanton was recruited sixth.
    (D)   Villas was recruited sixth.
    (E)   White was recruited third.

4. If Quinn was recruited immediately before Rovero, then Stanton CANNOT have been recruited

    (A)   first
    (B)   second
    (C)   third
    (D)   fifth
    (E)   seventh

5. If White was recruited earlier than Rovero and if Rovero was recruited earlier than Tao, then which one of the following could be true?

    (A)   Quinn was recruited first.
    (B)   Rovero was recruited third.
    (C)   Stanton was recruited second.
    (D)   Tao was recruited sixth.
    (E)   Villas was recruited sixth.

6. If White was recruited immediately before Quinn, which one of the following must have been recruited sixth?

    (A)   Quinn
    (B)   Rovero
    (C)   Stanton
    (D)   Villas
    (E)   White

GO ON TO THE NEXT PAGE.

Questions 7–13

In the Lifestyle, Metro, and Sports sections of tomorrow's newspaper, a total of six different photographs are to appear, exactly two photographs per section. Each of the available photographs was taken by one of three photographers: Fuentes, Gagnon, and Hue. Selection of the photographs is constrained by the following conditions:

> For each photographer, at least one but no more than three of that photographer's photographs must appear.
> At least one photograph in the Lifestyle section must be by a photographer who has at least one photograph in the Metro section.
> The number of Hue's photographs in the Lifestyle section must be the same as the number of Fuentes' photographs in the Sports section.
> None of Gagnon's photographs can be in the Sports section.

7. Which one of the following could be an acceptable selection of the photographs to appear?

(A)   Lifestyle: both photographs by Fuentes
        Metro: one photograph by Fuentes and one by Hue
        Sports: one photograph by Gagnon and one by Hue

(B)   Lifestyle: one photograph by Fuentes and one by Gagnon
        Metro: one photograph by Fuentes and one by Gagnon
        Sports: both photographs by Hue

(C)   Lifestyle: both photographs by Fuentes
        Metro: both photographs by Gagnon
        Sports: both photographs by Hue

(D)   Lifestyle: both photographs by Gagnon
        Metro: one photograph by Fuentes and one by Gagnon
        Sports: one photograph by Fuentes and one by Hue

(E)   Lifestyle: one photograph by Gagnon and one by Hue
        Metro: both photographs by Hue
        Sports: one photograph by Fuentes and one by Hue

GO ON TO THE NEXT PAGE.

8. If both photographs in the Lifestyle section are by Hue, then which one of the following must be true of the six photographs?

(A) Exactly one is by Fuentes.
(B) Exactly three are by Fuentes.
(C) Exactly one is by Gagnon.
(D) Exactly two are by Gagnon.
(E) Exactly two are by Hue.

9. If one photograph in the Lifestyle section is by Gagnon and one is by Hue, then which one of the following must be true?

(A) Exactly one photograph in the Metro section is by Fuentes.
(B) Exactly one photograph in the Metro section is by Gagnon.
(C) Both photographs in the Metro section are by Gagnon.
(D) Exactly one photograph in the Sports section is by Hue.
(E) Both photographs in the Sports section are by Hue.

10. Which one of the following could be true of the photographs by Fuentes appearing in tomorrow's paper?

(A) One is in the Lifestyle section, one is in the Metro section, and one is in the Sports section.
(B) One is in the Lifestyle section, and two are in the Sports section.
(C) Two are in the Lifestyle section, and one is in the Sports section.
(D) One is in the Metro section, and two are in the Sports section.
(E) Two are in the Metro section, and one is in the Sports section.

11. If one photograph in the Lifestyle section is by Fuentes and one is by Hue, then which one of the following could be true?

(A) Both photographs in the Metro section are by Fuentes.
(B) Both photographs in the Metro section are by Gagnon.
(C) Exactly one photograph in the Metro section is by Hue.
(D) Both photographs in the Sports section are by Hue.
(E) Neither photograph in the Sports section is by Hue.

12. If both photographs in one of the three sections are by Gagnon, then which one of the following could be true?

(A) Both photographs in the Lifestyle section are by Hue.
(B) One photograph in the Lifestyle section is by Fuentes and one is by Hue.
(C) Both photographs in the Metro section are by Fuentes.
(D) One photograph in the Metro section is by Gagnon and one is by Hue.
(E) Both photographs in the Sports section are by Hue.

13. If one photograph in the Metro section is by Fuentes and one is by Hue, then which one of the following could be true?

(A) Both photographs in the Lifestyle section are by Fuentes.
(B) Both photographs in the Lifestyle section are by Gagnon.
(C) One photograph in the Lifestyle section is by Gagnon and one is by Hue.
(D) Both photographs in the Lifestyle section are by Hue.
(E) Both photographs in the Sports section are by Fuentes.

GO ON TO THE NEXT PAGE.

Questions 14–18

Exactly five students—Grecia, Hakeem, Joe, Katya, and Louise—are to work at a campus art gallery during a special exhibit that runs for exactly five days, Monday through Friday. Each day is divided into two nonoverlapping shifts—first and second—with each student working exactly two shifts. Each shift is worked by exactly one of the students according to the following scheduling restrictions:

    No student works both shifts of any day.
    On two consecutive days, Louise works the second shift.
    On two nonconsecutive days, Grecia works the first shift.
    Katya works on Tuesday and Friday.
    Hakeem and Joe work on the same day as each other at least once.
    Grecia and Louise never work on the same day as each other.

14. Which one of the following could be the list of the students who work the second shifts at the gallery, in order from Monday through Friday?

(A)   Hakeem, Louise, Louise, Hakeem, Katya
(B)   Joe, Hakeem, Grecia, Louise, Louise
(C)   Joe, Katya, Hakeem, Louise, Katya
(D)   Louise, Katya, Joe, Louise, Katya
(E)   Louise, Louise, Hakeem, Joe, Joe

GO ON TO THE NEXT PAGE.

15. Which one of the following must be true?

   (A)   Grecia does not work at the gallery on
         Tuesday.
   (B)   Hakeem does not work at the gallery on
         Wednesday.
   (C)   Joe does not work at the gallery on Tuesday.
   (D)   Joe does not work at the gallery on Thursday.
   (E)   Louise does not work at the gallery on
         Tuesday.

16. If Hakeem works at the gallery on Wednesday, then
   Joe must work at the gallery on which one of the
   following pairs of days?

   (A)   Monday and Wednesday
   (B)   Monday and Thursday
   (C)   Tuesday and Wednesday
   (D)   Tuesday and Thursday
   (E)   Wednesday and Thursday

17. If there is at least one day on which Grecia and Joe
   both work at the gallery, then which one of the
   following could be true?

   (A)   Grecia works the first shift on Tuesday.
   (B)   Hakeem works the second shift on Monday.
   (C)   Hakeem works the second shift on
         Wednesday.
   (D)   Joe works the first shift on Wednesday.
   (E)   Joe works the first shift on Thursday.

18. If Katya works the second shift on Tuesday at the
   gallery, then which one of the following could be true?

   (A)   Grecia works the first shift on Monday.
   (B)   Hakeem works the first shift on Monday.
   (C)   Hakeem works the second shift on Wednesday.
   (D)   Joe works the second shift on Thursday.
   (E)   Louise works the second shift on Monday.

GO ON TO THE NEXT PAGE.

Questions 19–23

A publisher is planning to publish six cookbooks—K, L, M, N, O, and P—over the course of the next year. Each cookbook will be published in one of two seasons—fall or spring—subject to the following conditions:

M and P cannot be published in the same season as each other.

K and N must be published in the same season as each other.

If K is published in the fall, O must also be published in the fall.

If M is published in the fall, N must be published in the spring.

19. Which one of the following is an acceptable schedule for the publication of the cookbooks?

(A) fall: K, L, M, and O
spring: N and P

(B) fall: K, L, N, and O
spring: M and P

(C) fall: K, L, N, and P
spring: M and O

(D) fall: K, M, N, and O
spring: L and P

(E) fall: M and O
spring: K, L, N, and P

GO ON TO THE NEXT PAGE.

20. If M is published in the fall, which one of the following is a pair of cookbooks that could both be published in the fall along with M?

    (A) K and O
    (B) L and N
    (C) L and O
    (D) N and P
    (E) O and P

21. If N is published in the fall, which one of the following could be true?

    (A) K is published in the spring.
    (B) L is published in the fall.
    (C) M is published in the fall.
    (D) O is published in the spring.
    (E) P is published in the spring.

22. The schedule for the publication of the cookbooks is fully determined if which one of the following is true?

    (A) K is published in the fall and L is published in the spring.
    (B) O is published in the fall and P is published in the spring.
    (C) P is published in the fall and L is published in the spring.
    (D) Both K and L are published in the spring.
    (E) Both M and L are published in the fall.

23. Which one of the following, if substituted for the condition that if M is published in the fall, N must be published in the spring, would have the same effect in determining the schedule for the publication of the cookbooks?

    (A) If L is published in the fall, M must be published in the spring.
    (B) If N is published in the fall, P must also be published in the fall.
    (C) If M is published in the spring, P must be published in the fall.
    (D) If N is published in the spring, M must also be published in the spring.
    (E) If O is published in the spring, N must also be published in the spring.

S T O P

IF YOU FINISH BEFORE TIME IS CALLED, YOU MAY CHECK YOUR WORK ON THIS SECTION ONLY.
DO NOT WORK ON ANY OTHER SECTION IN THE TEST.

SECTION IV
Time—35 minutes
25 Questions

Directions: The questions in this section are based on the reasoning contained in brief statements or passages. For some questions, more than one of the choices could conceivably answer the question. However, you are to choose the best answer; that is, the response that most accurately and completely answers the question. You should not make assumptions that are by commonsense standards implausible, superfluous, or incompatible with the passage. After you have chosen the best answer, blacken the corresponding space on your answer sheet.

1. Aisha: Vadim is going to be laid off. Vadim's work as a programmer has been exemplary since joining the firm. But management has already made the decision to lay off a programmer. And this firm strictly follows a policy of laying off the most recently hired programmer in such cases.

    Aisha's conclusion follows logically if which one of the following is assumed?

    (A)   The firm values experience in its programmers more highly than any other quality.
    (B)   When Vadim was hired, the policy of laying off the most recently hired programmer was clearly explained.
    (C)   Vadim is the most recently hired programmer at the firm.
    (D)   Every other programmer at the firm has done better work than Vadim.
    (E)   It is bad policy that the firm always lays off the most recently hired programmer.

2. Wanda: It is common sense that one cannot create visual art without visual stimuli in one's work area, just as a writer needs written stimuli. A stark, empty work area would hinder my creativity. This is why there are so many things in my studio.

    Vernon: But a writer needs to read good writing, not supermarket tabloids. Are you inspired by the piles of laundry and empty soda bottles in your studio?

    Which one of the following most accurately expresses the principle underlying Vernon's response to Wanda?

    (A)   It is unhealthy to work in a cluttered work area.
    (B)   The quality of the stimuli in an artist's environment matters.
    (C)   Supermarket tabloids should not be considered stimulating.
    (D)   Messiness impairs artistic creativity.
    (E)   One should be able to be creative even in a stark, empty work area.

3. The official listing of an animal species as endangered triggers the enforcement of legal safeguards designed to protect endangered species, such as tighter animal export and trade restrictions and stronger antipoaching laws. Nevertheless, there have been many cases in which the decline in the wild population of a species was more rapid after that species was listed as endangered than before it was so listed.

    Which one of the following, if true, does most to account for the increase in the rate of population decline described above?

    (A)   The process of officially listing a species as endangered can take many years.
    (B)   Public campaigns to save endangered animal species often focus only on those species that garner the public's affection.
    (C)   The number of animal species listed as endangered has recently increased dramatically.
    (D)   Animals are more desirable to collectors when they are perceived to be rare.
    (E)   Poachers find it progressively more difficult to locate animals of a particular species as that species' population declines.

4. Annette: To persuade the town council to adopt your development plan, you should take them on a trip to visit other towns that have successfully implemented plans like yours.

    Sefu: But I have a vested interest in their votes. If council members were to accept a trip from me, it would give the appearance of undue influence.

    The dialogue provides the most support for the claim that Annette and Sefu disagree over whether

    (A)   the council should adopt Sefu's development plan
    (B)   Sefu should take the council on a trip to visit other towns
    (C)   Sefu has a vested interest in the council's votes
    (D)   other towns have successfully implemented similar development plans
    (E)   the appearance of undue influence should be avoided

GO ON TO THE NEXT PAGE.

5. Scholar: Recently, some religions have updated the language of their traditional texts and replaced traditional rituals with more contemporary ones. These changes have been followed by increases in attendance at places of worship affiliated with these religions. This shows that any such modernization will result in increased numbers of worshipers.

The scholar's reasoning is flawed because the scholar presumes without giving sufficient justification that

(A) not every religion can update its texts and replace its traditional rituals

(B) modernization of religious texts and rituals will not involve an alteration of their messages

(C) the modernization of the texts and rituals of some religions was the cause of their increases in attendance

(D) making texts and rituals more modern is the only way in which a religion could bring about an increase in attendance at places of worship

(E) the growth in attendance at places of worship affiliated with religions that made their texts and rituals more modern is irreversible

6. If one is to participate in the regional band, one must practice very hard or be very talented. Therefore, Lily, who is first trombonist in the regional band and is very talented, does not practice hard.

The flawed reasoning in which one of the following arguments most closely resembles the flawed reasoning in the argument above?

(A) In order to have a chance to meet its objectives, the army needs good weather as a precondition for retaining its mobility. The weather is good today, so the army will meet its objectives.

(B) If Lois were on vacation, she would be visiting her brother in Chicago or seeing friends in Toronto. Since she is not on vacation, she is in neither Chicago nor Toronto.

(C) If Johnson is to win the local election, then neither Horan nor Jacobs can enter the race. Since neither of them plans to run, Johnson will win the race.

(D) To stay informed about current events, one must read a major newspaper or watch national TV news every day. So Julie, who is informed about current events and reads a major newspaper every day, does not watch TV news.

(E) If Wayne is to get a ride home from the library, either Yvette or Marty must be there. Yvette is not at the library, so Marty must be there.

7. Dietitian: Eating fish can lower one's cholesterol level. In a study of cholesterol levels and diet, two groups were studied. The first group ate a balanced diet including two servings of fish per week. The second group ate a very similar diet, but ate no fish. The first group showed lower cholesterol levels, on average, than the second group. The two groups had displayed similar average cholesterol levels prior to the study.

Which one of the following most accurately describes the role played in the dietitian's argument by the claim that the two groups had displayed similar average cholesterol levels prior to the study?

(A) It is offered as an objection to the main conclusion of the argument.

(B) It expresses the main conclusion of the argument.

(C) It rules out an alternative explanation of the data collected in the study.

(D) It provides background information on the purpose of the study.

(E) It introduces an alternative explanation of the phenomenon described in the main conclusion.

8. Satellite navigation systems (satnavs) for cars, in which computer voices announce directions as you drive, save fuel and promote safety. Studies show that, when assigned to novel destinations, drivers using satnavs took, on average, 7 percent fewer miles per journey than drivers using paper maps. Fewer miles driven means, on average, less fuel consumed. Also, the drivers who used satnavs drove more carefully in that they were not taking their eyes off the road to check paper maps.

Which one of the following, if true, most strengthens the argument?

(A) People who are often required to drive to novel destinations are more likely to use satnavs than people who are rarely required to drive to novel destinations.

(B) The more fuel a vehicle consumes, the more motivation a driver has to find the shortest route to his or her destination.

(C) Drivers who do not routinely need to drive to an unfamiliar location are more likely to plan out their route carefully prior to departure.

(D) Drivers who own satnavs usually prefer to drive to their accustomed destinations by using their customary routes rather than by following the directions given by the satnavs.

(E) Drivers who are given directions as needed are less likely to change course suddenly or make other risky maneuvers.

GO ON TO THE NEXT PAGE.

9. A manager cannot extract the best performance from employees by threatening them with termination or offering financial rewards for high productivity. Rather, employees must come to want to do a good job for its own sake. One of the best ways for a manager to achieve this is to delegate responsibility to them, especially for decisions that previously had to be made by the manager.

Which one of the following propositions is best illustrated by the situation described in the passage?

(A) Increased responsibility can improve a person's sense of how power should be used.
(B) It is often the case that the desire for prestige is more powerful than the desire for job security.
(C) In some cases one's effectiveness in a particular role can be enhanced by a partial relinquishing of control.
(D) People who carry out decisions are in the best position to determine what those decisions should be.
(E) Business works best by harnessing the self-interest of individuals to benefit the company as a whole.

10. Richard: Because it fails to meet the fundamental requirement of art—that it represent—abstract art will eventually be seen as an aberration.

Jung-Su: Although artists, like musicians, may reject literal representation, makers of abstract art choose to represent the purely formal features of objects, which are discovered only when everyday perspectives are rejected. Thus, whatever others might come to say, abstract art is part of the artistic mainstream.

Richard and Jung-Su disagree over whether

(A) makers of abstract art reject literal representation
(B) the fundamental requirement of art is that it represent
(C) musicians may reject literal representation
(D) abstract art will be seen as an aberration
(E) abstract art is representational

11. A person who knowingly brings about misfortune should be blamed for it. However, in some cases a person who unwittingly brings about misfortune should not be blamed for it. For example, a person should never be blamed for unwittingly bringing about misfortune if the person could not reasonably have foreseen it.

The principles above, if valid, most help to justify the reasoning in which one of the following?

(A) Although he would have realized it if he had thought about it, it did not occur to Riley that parking his car in the center lane of Main Street could lead to a traffic accident. So, if a traffic accident does result from Riley's parking his car in the center lane of Main Street, he should not be blamed for it.
(B) Oblicek had no idea that suggesting to her brother that he take out a loan to expand his business was likely to cause the business to go bankrupt, nor could she have reasonably foreseen this. So, if the loan does cause her brother's business to go bankrupt, Oblicek should not be blamed for it.
(C) Gougon had no reason to think that serving the hollandaise sauce would make his guests ill, but he was concerned that it might. Thus, if the hollandaise sauce does make Gougon's guests ill, Gougon should be blamed for it.
(D) When Dr. Fitzpatrick gave his patient the wrong medicine, he did not know that it would cause the patient to experience greatly increased blood pressure. So, if no one else knowingly did anything that contributed to the patient's increase in blood pressure, no one other than Dr. Fitzpatrick is to blame for it.
(E) Any reasonable person could have foreseen that dropping a lit cigarette in dry leaves would start a fire. Thus, even if Kapp did not realize this, she is to blame for starting a fire on Rodriguez's farm since she dropped a lit cigarette in dry leaves there.

GO ON TO THE NEXT PAGE.

12. Researcher: Research has shown that inhaling the scent of lavender has measurable physiological effects tending to reduce stress. It is known that intense stress can impair the immune system, making one more susceptible to illness. Therefore, it is likely that the incidence of illness among those who regularly inhale the scent of lavender is reduced by this practice.

Which one of the following is an assumption that the researcher's argument requires?

(A) Many, if not all, of the scents that have a tendency to reduce susceptibility to illness do so, at least in part, by reducing stress.

(B) Some people who regularly inhale the scent of lavender would otherwise be under enough stress to impair their immune systems.

(C) At least some people who use the scent of lavender to induce relaxation and reduce stress are no more susceptible to illness than average.

(D) In anyone for whom the scent of lavender reduces susceptibility to illness, it does so primarily by reducing stress.

(E) Reduced stress diminishes susceptibility to illness only for people who are under enough stress to impair their immune systems to at least some degree.

13. Government statistics show that the real (adjusted for inflation) average income for families has risen over the last five years. Therefore, since this year the Andersen family's income is average for families, the family's real income must have increased over the last five years.

The reasoning in the argument is most vulnerable to criticism on the grounds that the argument

(A) ambiguously uses the term "average" in two different senses

(B) fails to take into account inflation with respect to the Andersen family's income

(C) overlooks the possibility that most families' incomes are below average

(D) fails to consider the possibility that the Andersen family's real income was above average in the recent past

(E) presumes, without providing justification, that the government makes no errors in gathering accurate estimates of family income

14. Certain methods of creating high-quality counterfeit banknotes involve making accurate measurements of the images printed on genuine banknotes. Hence, if the production of high-quality counterfeit banknotes is to be prevented, some of the images on banknotes must be made very difficult or impossible to measure accurately.

The argument's conclusion can be properly drawn if which one of the following is assumed?

(A) Today's copying technology is sophisticated enough to replicate almost any paper product with great precision.

(B) Once the images printed on a banknote have been measured accurately, there is no further impediment to the banknote's being exactly replicated.

(C) Governments have better printing technology available to them than counterfeiters do.

(D) Few countries produce banknotes with images that are difficult for counterfeiters to measure accurately.

(E) New designs in banknotes generally lead to decreases in the amount of counterfeit currency in circulation.

15. Armstrong: For the treatment of a particular disease, Dr. Sullivan argues for using nutritional supplements rather than the pharmaceuticals that most doctors prescribe. But this is in his self-interest since he is paid to endorse a line of nutritional supplements. Thus, we should not use nutritional supplements in treating the disease.

Armstrong's argument is flawed in that it

(A) relies on two different meanings of the term "supplement" to draw a conclusion

(B) relies solely on an appeal to an authority whose trustworthiness should not necessarily be taken for granted

(C) appeals to people's emotions regarding the treatment of disease rather than to the efficacy of the two approaches to treatment

(D) criticizes Dr. Sullivan's motives for holding a position rather than addressing the position itself

(E) fails to justify its presumption that nutritional supplements cannot be used in conjunction with other treatments

GO ON TO THE NEXT PAGE.

16. Economist: If the economy grows stronger, employment will increase, and hence more parents will need to find day care for their young children. Unfortunately, in a stronger economy many day-care workers will quit to take better-paying jobs in other fields. Therefore, a stronger economy is likely to make it much more difficult to find day care.

Which one of the following is an assumption the economist's argument requires?

(A) If the economy grows stronger, most of the new jobs that are created will be in fields that pay well.

(B) If the economy grows stronger, the number of new day-care workers will not be significantly greater than the number of day-care workers who move to better-paying jobs in other fields.

(C) If the economy grows stronger, the number of workers employed by day-care centers is likely to decrease.

(D) The shortage of day care for children is unlikely to worsen unless employment increases and many day-care center employees quit to take better-paying jobs in other fields.

(E) The total number of young children in day-care centers will decrease if the cost of day care increases significantly.

17. Ostrich farming requires far less acreage than cattle ranching requires, and ostriches reproduce much faster than cattle. Starting out in cattle ranching requires a large herd of cows, one bull, and at least two acres per cow. By contrast, two pairs of yearling ostriches and one acre of similar land are enough to begin ostrich farming. The start-up costs for ostrich farming are greater, but it can eventually bring in as much as five times what cattle ranching does.

Which one of the following is most strongly supported by the information above?

(A) Two pairs of yearling ostriches are more expensive than a herd of cows and a bull.

(B) Cattle ranching is not a good source of income.

(C) A cow consumes no more feed than an ostrich does.

(D) The average ostrich farm generates almost five times as much profit as the average cattle ranch.

(E) Ostrich farmers typically lose money during their first year.

18. For several centuries there have been hairless dogs in western Mexico and in coastal Peru. It is very unlikely that a trait as rare as hairlessness emerged on two separate occasions. Since the dogs have never existed in the wild, and the vast mountainous jungle separating these two regions would have made overland travel between them extremely difficult centuries ago, the dogs must have been transported from one of these regions to the other by boat, probably during trading expeditions.

Which one of the following is an assumption that the argument requires?

(A) Hairless dogs have never been found anywhere except in the regions of western Mexico and coastal Peru.

(B) Most of the trade goods that came into western Mexico centuries ago were transported by boat.

(C) Centuries ago, no one would have traveled between western Mexico and coastal Peru by boat except for the purposes of carrying out a trading expedition.

(D) If hairless dogs were at one time transported between western Mexico and coastal Peru by boat, they were traded in exchange for other goods.

(E) Centuries ago, it was easier to travel by boat between western Mexico and coastal Peru than to travel by an overland route.

19. Researchers working in Western Australia have discovered the oldest fragments of the Earth's early crust that have yet been identified: microdiamonds. These microscopic crystals measure only 50 microns across and were formed 4.2 billion years ago. This discovery sheds light on how long it took for the Earth's crust to form, since this date is only 300 million years after the formation of the Earth itself.

If the statements above are true, which one of the following must also be true?

(A) The Earth's crust took no longer than 300 million years to start to form.

(B) The Earth's crust first formed in the area that is now Western Australia.

(C) The Earth's crust took billions of years to form.

(D) Microdiamonds were the first components of the Earth's crust to form.

(E) All naturally occurring microdiamonds were formed at the time the Earth's crust was being formed.

GO ON TO THE NEXT PAGE.

20. The public square was an important tool of democracy in days past because it provided a forum for disparate citizens to discuss the important issues of the day. Today, a person with Internet access can discuss important issues with millions of people across the nation, allowing the Internet to play the role once played by the public square. Hence, we should ensure that Internet users have at least as much freedom of expression as did people speaking in the public square.

Which one of the following is an assumption required by the argument?

(A) People speaking in the public square of days past had complete freedom of expression.

(B) All citizens have the same level of access to the Internet.

(C) A public forum can lose effectiveness as a tool of democracy if participants cannot discuss issues freely.

(D) The Internet is more often used to discuss important issues than to discuss frivolous issues.

(E) Other than the Internet, no other public forum today is an important tool of democracy.

21. At a large elementary school researchers studied a small group of children who successfully completed an experimental program in which they learned to play chess. The study found that most of the children who completed the program soon showed a significant increase in achievement levels in all of their schoolwork. Thus, it is likely that the reasoning power and spatial intuition exercised in chess-playing also contribute to achievement in many other areas of intellectual activity.

Which one of the following, if true, most tends to undermine the argument?

(A) Some students who did not participate in the chess program had learned to play chess at home.

(B) Those children who began the program but who did not successfully complete it had lower preprogram levels of achievement than did those who eventually did successfully complete the program.

(C) Many of the children who completed the program subsequently sought membership on a school chess team that required a high grade average for membership.

(D) Some students who did not participate in the chess program participated instead in after-school study sessions that helped them reach much higher levels of achievement in the year after they attended the sessions.

(E) At least some of the students who did not successfully complete the program were nevertheless more talented chess players than some of the students who did complete the program.

GO ON TO THE NEXT PAGE.

22. On Wednesdays, Kate usually buys some guava juice. But the only place she can buy guava juice is the local health food store. It follows that she must sometimes shop at the local health food store on Wednesdays.

The argument above is most similar in its pattern of reasoning to which one of the following arguments?

(A) Only teachers at the Culinary Institute are allowed to use the institute's main kitchen. Most dinners at Cafe Delice are prepared in that kitchen. So at least some dinners at Cafe Delice must be prepared by Culinary Institute teachers.

(B) All dinners at Cafe Delice are prepared in the main kitchen of the Culinary Institute. But only teachers at the institute are allowed to use that kitchen. So the dinners at Cafe Delice must be prepared by Culinary Institute teachers.

(C) Most dinners at Cafe Delice are prepared in the main kitchen of the Culinary Institute. All the teachers at the institute are allowed to use that kitchen. So at least some dinners at Cafe Delice must be prepared by Culinary Institute teachers.

(D) Most teachers at the Culinary Institute are allowed to use the institute's main kitchen. Dinners at Cafe Delice are only prepared in that kitchen. So dinners at Cafe Delice must sometimes be prepared by Culinary Institute teachers.

(E) Only teachers at the Culinary Institute are allowed to use the main kitchen of the institute. Dinners at Cafe Delice are usually prepared by Culinary Institute teachers. So dinners at Cafe Delice must sometimes be prepared in the main kitchen of the Culinary Institute.

23. Editor: The city's previous recycling program, which featured pickup of recyclables every other week, was too costly. The city claims that its new program, which features weekly pickup, will be more cost effective, since the greater the volume of recyclables collected per year, the more revenue the city gains from selling the recyclables. But this is absurd. People will put out the same volume of recyclables overall; it will just be spread out over a greater number of pickups.

Which one of the following, if true, most weakens the editor's argument?

(A) The cost of collecting and disposing of general trash has been less than the cost of collecting and disposing of recyclables, and this is still likely to be the case under the new recycling program.

(B) Even if the volume of collected recyclables increases, that increase might not be enough to make the recycling program cost effective.

(C) Because the volume of recyclables people accumulate during a week is less than what they accumulate during two weeks, the city expects a recyclables pickup to take less time under the new program.

(D) A weekly schedule for recyclables pickup is substantially easier for people to follow and adhere to than is a schedule of pickups every other week.

(E) Because of the increase in the number of pickups under the new program, the amount charged by the contractor that collects the city's recyclables will increase significantly.

GO ON TO THE NEXT PAGE.

24. Professor: Many introductory undergraduate science courses are intended to be "proving grounds," that is, they are designed to be so demanding that only those students most committed to being science majors will receive passing grades in these courses. However, studies show that some of the students in these very demanding introductory courses who are least enthusiastic about science receive passing grades in these courses. Hence, designing introductory science courses to serve as proving grounds has not served its intended purpose.

Which one of the following is an assumption that the professor's argument requires?

(A) If some of the students who are most enthusiastic about science do not receive passing grades in introductory science courses, then designing these courses to serve as proving grounds has been unsuccessful.

(B) Science departments need a way to ensure that only those students most committed to being science majors will receive passing grades in introductory science courses.

(C) Some of the students in the very demanding introductory science courses who are most enthusiastic about science do not receive passing grades in those courses.

(D) None of the students in the very demanding introductory science courses who are least enthusiastic about science are among the students most committed to being science majors.

(E) Introductory science courses should not continue to be designed to serve as proving grounds if doing so has not served its intended purpose.

25. Many bird and reptile species use hissing as a threat device against potential predators. The way these species produce hissing sounds is similar enough that it is likely that this behavior developed in an early common ancestor. At the time this common ancestor would have lived, however, none of its potential predators would have yet acquired the anatomy necessary to hear hissing sounds.

Which one of the following, if true, most helps to resolve the apparent discrepancy in the information above?

(A) Like its potential predators, the common ancestor of bird and reptile species would have lacked the anatomy necessary to hear hissing sounds.

(B) The common ancestor of bird and reptile species would probably have employed multiple threat devices against potential predators.

(C) The production of a hissing sound would have increased the apparent body size of the common ancestor of bird and reptile species.

(D) The use of hissing as a threat device would have been less energetically costly than other threat behaviors available to the common ancestor of bird and reptile species.

(E) Unlike most modern bird and reptile species, the common ancestor of these species would have had few predators.

S T O P

IF YOU FINISH BEFORE TIME IS CALLED, YOU MAY CHECK YOUR WORK ON THIS SECTION ONLY.
DO NOT WORK ON ANY OTHER SECTION IN THE TEST.

Wait for the supervisor's instructions before you open the page to the topic.
Please print and sign your name and write the date in the designated spaces below.
Time: 35 Minutes

General Directions

You will have 35 minutes in which to plan and write an essay on the topic inside. Read the topic and the accompanying directions carefully. You will probably find it best to spend a few minutes considering the topic and organizing your thoughts before you begin writing. In your essay, be sure to develop your ideas fully, leaving time, if possible, to review what you have written. **Do not write on a topic other than the one specified. Writing on a topic of your own choice is not acceptable.**

No special knowledge is required or expected for this writing exercise. Law schools are interested in the reasoning, clarity, organization, language usage, and writing mechanics displayed in your essay. How well you write is more important than how much you write.

Confine your essay to the blocked, lined area on the front and back of the separate Writing Sample Response Sheet. Only that area will be reproduced for law schools. Be sure that your writing is legible.

Both this topic sheet and your response sheet must be turned in to the testing staff before you leave the room.

Topic Code
134262

Date
/   /

Print Your Full Name Here		
Last	First	M.I.

Sign Your Name Here

Scratch Paper
Do not write your essay in this space.

LSAT® Writing Sample Topic

Directions: The scenario presented below describes two choices, either one of which can be supported on the basis of the information given. Your essay should consider both choices and argue for one over the other, based on the two specified criteria and the facts provided. There is no "right" or "wrong" choice: a reasonable argument can be made for either.

Yasmin Parsi is deciding whether to cast an unknown actor to star in her new studio film or to hire Jonathan Tauzen, an actor with many fans. Using the facts below, write an essay in which you argue for one choice over the other, based on the following two criteria:

- Parsi wants to have as much creative control over her film as possible.
- Parsi wants to make it as likely as possible that the studio will hire her to make another film in the future.

If a known star is not used, the studio will provide a minimal marketing budget and release the film in only a few markets. In the past the studio has given movies in limited release time to build an audience before deciding whether its investment was worthwhile. Though successful, Parsi's previous films were all independently produced with unknown actors. Under her current deal, the studio retains some control over the content of her film. The studio's history is to provide oversight in proportion to the amount of money it is contributing.

If Parsi hires Tauzen, the studio would provide extra funding to cover the cost of an established star. The studio would also provide a moderate publicity budget to allow for a wide release of the film. The studio has a history of abandoning movies in wide release if they do not quickly become popular. With a known actor there would be pressure from both the studio and the actor to make the actor's part more central to the film. Tauzen could be an effective ally if Parsi has other creative differences with the studio. Tauzen has a history of causing delays in filming. This has sometimes led to the films going over budget.

WP-W134A

Scratch Paper
Do not write your essay in this space.

LAST
NAME
(Print)

FIRST
NAME
(Print)

LAST 4 DIGITS OF SOCIAL
SECURITY/SOCIAL
INSURANCE NO.

L

⓪	⓪	⓪	⓪	⓪	⓪	⓪	⓪
①	①	①	①	①	①	①	①
②	②	②	②	②	②	②	②
③	③	③	③	③	③	③	③
④	④	④	④	④	④	④	④
⑤	⑤	⑤	⑤	⑤	⑤	⑤	⑤
⑥	⑥	⑥	⑥	⑥	⑥	⑥	⑥
⑦	⑦	⑦	⑦	⑦	⑦	⑦	⑦
⑧	⑧	⑧	⑧	⑧	⑧	⑧	⑧
⑨	⑨	⑨	⑨	⑨	⑨	⑨	⑨

LSAC ACCOUNT NO.

MI

TEST
CENTER NO.

SIGNATURE

M M D D Y Y
TEST DATE

Writing Sample Response Sheet

DO NOT WRITE
IN THIS SPACE

Begin your essay in the lined area below.
Continue on the back if you need more space.

⓪	⓪	⓪	⓪	⓪	⓪
①	①	①	①	①	①
②	②	②	②	②	②
③	③	③	③	③	③
④	④	④	④	④	④
⑤	⑤	⑤	⑤	⑤	⑤
⑥	⑥	⑥	⑥	⑥	⑥
⑦	⑦	⑦	⑦	⑦	⑦
⑧	⑧	⑧	⑧	⑧	⑧
⑨	⑨	⑨	⑨	⑨	⑨

TOPIC CODE

COMPUTING YOUR SCORE

Directions:

1. Use the Answer Key on the next page to check your answers.

2. Use the Scoring Worksheet below to compute your raw score.

3. Use the Score Conversion Chart to convert your raw score into the 120–180 scale.

Scoring Worksheet

1. Enter the number of questions you answered correctly in each section.

	Number Correct
SECTION I.................	_____
SECTION II................	_____
SECTION III..............	_____
SECTION IV	_____

2. Enter the sum here: _____

   This is your Raw Score.

Conversion Chart
For Converting Raw Score to the 120–180 LSAT Scaled Score
LSAT Form 5LSN115

Reported Score	Raw Score Lowest	Raw Score Highest
180	99	101
179	98	98
178	97	97
177	96	96
176	95	95
175	94	94
174	93	93
173	92	92
172	91	91
171	90	90
170	89	89
169	87	88
168	86	86
167	84	85
166	83	83
165	82	82
164	80	81
163	78	79
162	77	77
161	75	76
160	73	74
159	72	72
158	70	71
157	68	69
156	66	67
155	65	65
154	63	64
153	61	62
152	59	60
151	58	58
150	56	57
149	54	55
148	53	53
147	51	52
146	49	50
145	48	48
144	46	47
143	44	45
142	43	43
141	41	42
140	40	40
139	38	39
138	37	37
137	35	36
136	34	34
135	33	33
134	31	32
133	30	30
132	28	29
131	27	27
130	26	26
129	25	25
128	23	24
127	22	22
126	21	21
125	20	20
124	19	19
123	17	18
122	16	16
121	*	*
120	0	15

*There is no raw score that will produce this scaled score for this form.

ANSWER KEY

SECTION I

1.	C	8.	B	15.	E	22.	C
2.	B	9.	B	16.	C	23.	D
3.	D	10.	C	17.	C	24.	B
4.	A	11.	B	18.	B	25.	A
5.	D	12.	D	19.	E	26.	B
6.	A	13.	D	20.	C	27.	E
7.	D	14.	B	21.	C		

SECTION II

1.	B	8.	E	15.	A	22.	A
2.	B	9.	B	16.	C	23.	E
3.	C	10.	B	17.	D	24.	D
4.	C	11.	A	18.	B	25.	D
5.	C	12.	B	19.	C	26.	E
6.	D	13.	D	20.	E		
7.	C	14.	E	21.	B		

SECTION III

1.	D	8.	C	15.	C	22.	A
2.	C	9.	D	16.	B	23.	B
3.	D	10.	A	17.	E		
4.	B	11.	C	18.	B		
5.	A	12.	E	19.	E		
6.	B	13.	C	20.	C		
7.	B	14.	A	21.	B		

SECTION IV

1.	C	8.	E	15.	D	22.	A
2.	B	9.	C	16.	B	23.	D
3.	D	10.	E	17.	A	24.	D
4.	B	11.	B	18.	E	25.	C
5.	C	12.	B	19.	A		
6.	D	13.	D	20.	C		
7.	C	14.	B	21.	C		